THE QUAKER PEACE EDUCATION PROJECT 1988-1994

DEVELOPING UNTRIED STRATEGIES

by

JERRY TYRRELL

D1471690

**Centre for the Study of Conflict
University of Ulster**

The Quaker Peace Education Project 1988-1994:
Developing Untried Strategies
by
Jerry Tyrrell

Centre for the Study of Conflict
University of Ulster at Coleraine

ISBN 1 85923 007 5

Printed by University of Ulster

Acknowledgements

The author is glad to acknowledge the interest, cooperation and help of all those who agreed to be interviewed. I would like to thank all the staff and volunteers involved in the QPEP team, management committee and the Ulster Quaker Peace Committee who sponsored the project.

I would also like to thank Professor John Darby and Professor Seamus Dunn and staff at the Centre for the Study of Conflict for their advice and assistance.

I am grateful to Sharon Moran and Ruth McIlwaine for their assistance in preparing the final typescript, and also the following for their advice, help and critical comments during the drafting of this report; Cherie Brown, Seamus Dunn, Seamus Farrell, Marty Lynn and Hugh O'Doherty.

The interpretations put upon interview data and the content and structure of this final version of the report are, of course, the responsibility of the author alone.

Preface

The Centre for the Study of Conflict is a research centre based in the University of Ulster. Its main work is the promotion and encouragement of research on the community conflict and to this end it concentrates on practical issues to do with institutional and community structures and change. It publishes papers and books arising out of this work including: a series of research papers particularly designed to make available research data and reports; a series of Majority-Minority reports and a series of occasional papers by distinguished academics in the field of conflict.

This report is a new publication by Jerry Tyrrell on The Quaker Peace Education Project, 1988-1994, which looks specifically at the role of QPEP in bringing peace education into the classroom. The report investigates adult and child education and the important role which teachers have to play in the process of peace-making.

This is one of a set of new publications which the Centre will produce over the next few months on topics such as Parades, the Role of the Police, Classroom Mediation and Sport and Community Relations in Northern Ireland.

Seamus Dunn
June 1995

CONTENTS

Introduction   1

Chapter 1   The Global Context   6

Chapter 2   Development of the QPEP Team and
             the Workshop Approach   10

Chapter 3   Getting into Schools   17

Chapter 4   Influences and Initiatives   26

Chapter 5   Action Research   32

Chapter 6   International Work   37

Chapter 7   Adult Education Work   41

Chapter 8   Seeds of Resistance   47

Chapter 9   Transition from the First Phase
             to the Second Phase   55

Chapter 10   Work with Children and Young People   60

Chapter 11   Involving Teachers More Closely in the Work   66

Chapter 12   Training and Role of the QPEP Team   76

Chapter 13   The European Network for Conflict Resolution
             in Education, Summer School   81

Chapter 14   The Role of QPEP in the Development of the
             Work of the NCBI in Northern Ireland   86

Chapter 15   The Charities Evaluation Services
             Evaluation of the QPEP   99

Chapter 16   The Pilot Peer Mediation Project   108

Chapter 17   Building on Firm Foundations   118

INTRODUCTION

The Quaker Peace Education Project (QPEP) was born out of a challenge at a 1984 conference organised by the Ulster Quaker Peace Committee (UQPC).

> Given our commitment to the Quaker Peace Testimony, what were we (Quakers) doing actively to promote peace and understanding in the community?[1]

The response from the conference was a recommendation that UQPC become involved in peace education, and a working party was set up to explore the feasibility.

Ulster Quaker Peace Committee was active in organising conferences, and other events, but had never taken on anything as ambitious as the Peace Education Project was to turn out to be. As John Lampen points out, there was a perspective that UQPC being

> a relatively old institution and a fairly conservative one, ... there were many Friends (Quakers) in the early '70s who were .. dissatisfied with the responses (of UQPC) to the outbreak of the Troubles.'[2]

The Ulster Quaker Service Committee (UQSC) by comparison adopted a much higher public profile, with its work at the Visitor's Centres at the Maze prison and at Maghaberry, and other social action projects. By the end of the 1970's UQSC had a substantial budget of tens of thousands of pounds, whereas UQPC had a minute annual budget.

A further constraint on UQPC was that there are at least two strands within the Society of Friends in N. Ireland, which sometimes have an uneasy relationship. The concern of the evangelical strand would be that the gospel be preached as part of any Quaker Project. The second, more liberal strand was represented by the social action projects undertaken by the UQSC.

A number of individuals played a key role in raising the sights of UQPC,

1

particularly its chairman Andrew Young who said,

> If we are going to get into this field, we need to meet those who
> are already involved in it and find out whether there is a gap for
> Quakers and what that gap is.[3]

The working party from the 1984 conference organised a one-day
conference in June 1985, to explore a possible role in peace education for
UQPC. Representatives of Education and Library Boards, University of
Ulster, Corrymeela, Community Relations in Schools (CRIS), Peace
People, Department of Education Northern Ireland, the Society of Friends,
and other agencies were invited. Sixteen people representing thirteen
agencies attended, in addition to the four members of the planning team,
and three members of the Quaker Peace Action Caravan (QPAC).

In a report of the conference in 'The Friendly Word' participants were
reported as having the view that the

> Quaker reputation for respecting the beliefs and attitudes of
> others would enable Quakers to play an important part in Educa-
> tion for Mutual Understanding. It would be appropriate for
> Quakers to become active in peace education because we are seen
> by the community at large as being independent and are respected
> as such. We could attempt to do things which other groups might
> find more difficult.[4]

> Andrew (Young) was rather surprised. 'I thought they might
> suggest that we ran a Peace Essay competition', he said to me, 'I
> wasn't expecting a hundred-thousand pound project. But we'll
> do it'.[5]

John Lampen[6] recalled ten years later that already a specific *Quaker* role
was being stressed, particularly in relation to teachers who were "afraid of,
or hostile to, EMU". There was an expressed need for a full-time paid
person, as apposed to ACE workers. The project shouldn't "be set up to
produce curriculum materials"; rather there was an emphasis on "interac-

tion with teachers." Because of work being done by the Peace Education Board in Belfast, it was felt there was more scope for this type of project in the North West.

There was general support from the conference; as regards the specifics the planning team started to "work away on what it could do, afterwards". In the same edition of the Friendly Word, the areas that the project would address and the functions it would perform were identified, and an appeal launched:-

Two areas which we feel should be addressed are to speak to the uncommitted and to support those who are committed but isolated. These aims will both involve extending the existing network of active people and co-ordinating what they are doing.

It is expected that a programme would develop performing some or all of the following functions:
* Collating and disseminating information on existing resources.
* Visiting schools and mounting events in schools in collaboration with teachers.
* Establishing on-going groups of like-minded teachers.
* Arranging the provision of skills-training for peace-educators.
* Providing a measure of consultancy and feed-back to established and developing ventures.
* Researching the effectiveness of strategies already being employed in peace education.
* Identifying and developing untried strategies.
* Seeking to enter into dialogue with those hostile to peace education.
*Liaising with other groups developing peace education.[7]

The idea of a link with the University of Ulster developed after the conference, largely on Andrew Young's initiative. Negotiations started between UQPC and UU and were protracted; originally UQPC wanted the field officer to be an UQPC employee within the University. This issue was resolved by setting up a Management Committee with four Quaker members, three University staff, and one representative of the Peace Education Board of the Irish Council of Churches and the Irish Commission of Justice and Peace (Education Board). A Quaker would chair the committee. This was a compromise that would "enable UQPC to honour its obligations to (those) who have financed the Project"[8] while foregoing its original intention of being the legal employer.

According to documents at the time, in discussions with potential funding bodies Ulster Quaker Peace Committee stressed that:

> 1) we were embarking upon a Quaker project, 2) that the work to be undertaken by the field worker would not be principally research but would be activities designed to develop peace education in schools.[9]

The project received substantial financial support from Quakers in Britain and Ireland.

> One in eight of all Quaker households in Ireland made contributions and one in five Quaker meetings in Ireland and Britain responded with donations.[10]

Although other sources including the Ireland Fund and the Commission of the European Communities provided funding, the bulk of donations were from Quaker individuals, Meetings and Trusts. By the time the staff was appointed in April 1988, sufficient funding had been raised by Andrew Young or promised for the first three years of the project. Once QPEP was set up, neither UQPC nor Andrew Young as its chairman, used its power to intervene.

The Trusts required UQPC to update them on the progress of the project, with the Joseph Rowntree Charitable Trust making it a condition of its grant that the project be periodically evaluated professionally - it has accepted that the overview of progress by members of the University will meet this need. [11] The day to day running of the project became the responsibility of the Management Committee, and the major contribution of UQPC was in raising the funds, and getting the project off the ground.

NOTES

1. "Ulster Quaker Peace Education Project". Paper prepared for the Management Committee of the Ulster Quaker Peace Education Project, by Ulster Quaker Peace Committee, March 1987.
2. Lampen, John, (1994) Interviewed by Jerry Tyrrell, Derry 3.3.94.
3. Ibid.
4. "New Quaker Initiative - Peace Education in N.I." The Friendly Word, March-April   1986.
5. "Annual Report 1992/93" (1993) Ulster Quaker Peace Education Project, Derry.
6. Lampen, John, Ibid.
7. "New Quaker Initiative - Peace Education in N.I.", Ibid.
8. "Ulster Quaker Peace Education Project", Ibid.
9. Ibid.
10. Ibid.
11. Ibid.

CHAPTER 1: THE GLOBAL CONTEXT

> The model of peace education which began to influence some
> teachers and others in N. Ireland owed much to American Quaker
> programmes in downtown New York and Philadelphia ..... Today's
> Quaker Peace Education Project ..... is certainly the most direct
> inheritor of that approach and ethos, but the concepts have been
> influential in aspects of the development of a wide range of other
> projects. [1]

As previously stated, from the outset the project was an overtly Quaker
one, and action rather than research orientated.

The Management Committee of the project was made up of individuals
with involvement and experience of research, peace studies, education for
mutual understanding, peace education and education generally.

Other influences on the early days of the project were the expertise and
experience of the staff and subsequent volunteer team. Their experience
in informal and social education, rather than formal or academic education,
reinforced the link with the more experiential approach to peace education
noted above.

I was appointed as fieldworker. As well as being a trained teacher I had
developed relevant expertise through being the Organiser of a children's
charity, Holiday Projects West. I had been instrumental in bringing Joyce
Davison of Children's Creative Response to Conflict (CCRC), New York,
to Northern Ireland in 1982 and 1983 to work with leaders and children in
cross-community residential programmes. CCRC had been established in
1972 by the New York Quaker Project on Community Conflict, which had
decided to adapt its nonviolent training programme to develop skills for
young people. CCRC activities were based on four central themes - Co-
Operation, Communication, Affirmation and Conflict Resolution. [2]

In 1984, Holiday Projects West invited four facilitators, two Jews and
two Palestinians from the Neve Shalom community in Israel to lead
workshops with Protestant and Catholic teenagers from Londonderry and
Limavady. Their approach was more confrontational and focussed on
conflict resolution than was the general trend in N. Ireland at the time.

> The distinguishing mark of these (intensive) workshops is that no
> attempt is made to avoid potentially contentious areas: rather
> participants learn that conflict can be dealt with constructively,
> using techniques of conflict resolution and confrontation
> resolution. [3]

In 1985 I had spent seven weeks on a Winston Churchill Travelling
Fellowship studying projects involving children and non-violence. This
visit had been largely inspired by the Manual on Non-violence and
Children, [4] published by Quakers in Philadelphia, which was also based
on the same four themes as CCRC. An interview with the Manual's editor,
Stephanie Judson, underscored the motivation behind the growing experiential peace education movement in the USA.

> The Non-violence and Children Programme began in the late 60's
> in the height of the Vietnam war. Many people in the United
> States, especially Quakers were eager to learn how to raise a
> generation of children nonviolently, that would change the situation
> in the future, and possibly prevent future Vietnams. [5]

There are parallels with the development of Education for Mutual
Understanding (EMU) in Northern Ireland. For example Richardson
argues in "EMU - Roots if not Wings"[6] that EMU was born out of a concern
to ensure that all children had the opportunity of learning about, and
meeting, children from "the other tradition" in N. Ireland.
   I visited a number of Quaker Schools in and around Philadelphia and
saw exercises in affirmation, co-operation, communication and conflict
resolution being incorporated into the daily curriculum.
   At the same time I became aware of the work of the Kingston Friends
Workshop Group (KFWG), through their manual "Ways and Means" [7]
KFWG like QPEP had been established as a result of an event organised
by Q-PAC. The Quaker Peace Action Caravan -

> was a mobile resource centre for peace education, (whose)
> function was to work with members of the Society of Friends

through established Quaker structures to reach the general public.[8]

Q-PAC was able to work in formal settings in schools, in Quaker meetings, and in street campaigning. For Sue Bowers, one of the founder members of KFWG and co-author of the "Ways and Means" manual, working in peace education in schools was a more attractive alternative to getting involved in street campaigning or protest as a witness for peace.

Sue Bowers was to become actively involved in QPEP's early development, her own background being one of youth work, "running a workshop was a bit like organising an adult leader training".[9] The influences on KFWG were the Manual on Non-violence and Children, and the Friendly Classroom for a Small Planet. [10]

John Lampen, who was to chair the Management Committee for four years and play an active role as a QPEP team member, also had international experience in Peace Education. He helped develop a programme for teachers in Uganda, basing his programme on the qualities underpinning peace education. He identified these as

> affirmation of oneself and others; giving and expecting of mutual respect; emphasising co-operation; remaining with conflicts till they are solved. [11]

Previous direct contact with experiential peace education in other settings was thus providing a context for the development of QPEP's methodology.

NOTES
1. Richardson, Norman, (1992) "Roots if Not Wings - Where did EMU come from?" Keynote Paper at the conference, 'EMU in Transition', Newcastle Co Down, 19th May 1992.
2. "Friendly Classroom Skills for Students and Teachers", leaflet about Children's Creative Response to Conflict (CCRC), Nyack, NJ, USA.
3. Mahon, Deirdre and Hinds, Joe, (1984) "Breaking through Barriers", An outline of an experiential reconciliation project. Leaflet. Holiday

Projects West, Derry.

4. Judson, Stephanie, (Ed) (1984) "Manual on Nonviolence and Children" New Society Publishers, Philadelphia Pa, USA.

5. Judson, Stephanie, (1985) Interviewed by Jerry Tyrrell, Philadelphia, 26th September 1985.

6. Richardson , Norman (1992) Ibid.

7. Bowers, Sue, (1984) "Ways and Means - An Approach to Problem Solving", Kingston Friends Workshop Group.

8. Merritt, Sandy, (Ed) (1987) "Speaking Our Peace - Exploring nonviolence and conflict resolution" Quaker Peace and Service, London.

9. Bowers, Sue, (1994) Interviewed by Jerry Tyrrell, the Hayes Conference Centre, Swanwick, Derbyshire, 22nd June 1994.

10. Prutzman et al, (1977) "The Friendly Classroom for a Small Planet" Quaker Project on Community Conflict, New York, NY.

11. Lampen, John, (1987) Kufundisha Amani - A Course in Peace Education for Teachers in Uganda, Institute of Teacher Education, KYAMBOGO, Kampala, Uganda.

CHAPTER 2: DEVELOPMENT OF THE QPEP TEAM AND THE WORKSHOP APPROACH

In April 1988 the Quaker Peace Education Project started as an action research project based at Magee College, attached to the Centre for the Study of Conflict at the University of Ulster, with myself as full-time paid Research Assistant with the role of field worker.

My remit was the area as outlined on page 3. A development within the first month was the formation of a team of volunteers. A proposal written in April 1988 described the aim, objective, duration of training, venue, intended participants, trainer, format and reporting procedure, of this team:-

The formation of a 'Q-PEP TEAM'.

Aim: To recruit and train a group of 6 - 8 volunteers in exercises in co-operation, communication, affirmation and conflict resolution exercises.

Objective: To create a team of people each of whom have a repertoire of games and exercises that they are familiar with, comfortable with, and aware of the theory and purpose of. [1]

The main resource was to be the "Ways and Means" manual. [2] Six morning training sessions were planned at weekly intervals, leading up to a workshop at a primary school. Although the I would be the trainer, there was an expectation that each participant would take on a leadership role.

When I was Organiser of Holiday Projects West, I'd made a local radio programme about my experiences in visiting projects involving children and nonviolence in the USA. [3] Two teachers, having heard the radio programme and being aware of the existence of the new project, made contact with me to explore the possibility of doing work in their schools. One was to meet with resistance, see page 17, the other arranged for the principal to invite the team in to do a workshop as part of this initial programme.

While the negotiations were going on for the workshop in the school, a team of people, most with considerable expertise in working with young people in informal settings, was recruited. A training programme was undertaken, with each training workshop planned, and evaluated. Letters were written to team members between meetings, with encouragement and reminding them to bring materials, or practise an exercise. To a greater or lesser extent the experience of a workshop was a new one for everybody. The evaluation of the first training workshop contained comments like,

> "I found talking about myself a bit embarrassing; but that is something I myself have to come to terms with", "Still not too clear on what we are trying to achieve", "Insufficient explanation of why we are doing things" were listed in the "What could have been improved" column. "What was good" however, elicited responses like, "not a classroom setting", "meeting each other", "new games", "learning a bit about the programme" and "small group where we will be able to listen and talk without feeling awkward". [4]

In my report of this first training workshop, I acknowledged that a number of issues had arisen about the "user-friendliness" of the exercises in particular and the workshop approach in general.

There was some resistance by one individual when the final exercise of the workshop was proposed, - a closing circle. The comment was made "are we charismatic?"

I was aware that the participants, who had had connections with the cross-community contact agency I'd previously worked with, were already

> "happy with the idea of affirmation, communication and co-operation and conflict resolution", whereas "the other person present was clear in saying that she felt that teachers/children would have difficulty with (the exercises)".

For her benefit at least, and to offset potential resistance there was a need for:-

> Clarity as to why the exercises, and workshop process, were being done; that the goal is not "for people to be nice to each other as a superfluous way of communicating. Rather (it is about) empowering young people to take control of their lives."

> - Stressing the collective experience of those present in using these ideas.

> - Requiring that

> if any person has any difficulty in doing these exercises, then it is okay for them to (acknowledge that) in the first person. Eg - 'I find this embarrassing', or 'I think this is over the top', rather than 'In normal education .....', or 'Teachers .....'.[5]

Each week the team tried out new exercises, for example experimenting with the use of puppets and songs, and reflected on their own experiences of school. Difficulties began to emerge, there was questioning of why we were doing this, "the negative attitude of one of our members", [6] and questions of "has enough thought been given to future input on 1. Problem solving?, 2. Handling confrontation?". [7]

This last point was responded to in week 5, where a "Goal Wish problem solving process" [8] was used to assist a team member deal with a domestic conflict. "Talking about the (problem)" and "Having a go at" this exercise were valued by the team members. [9]

By week four the "honeymoon" period was over; on the one hand individual team members had decided whether or not it was for them, and two had left. There was now a definite invitation to work in a school. This was instrumental in focussing the minds of the team, not least because the school workshop was to take place two weeks before originally planned.

A new sense of purpose was reflected in the evaluation comments in the fifth week of training. In answer to the question "What was good", some of the comments were, "Working out the timetable of events for the school visit," "Getting more clear about what is going to happen on the workshop and what we are aiming at." "Seeing that we are getting somewhere."[10] There was some concern expressed about "not knowing it well enough"[11] and that a team member hadn't shown up, and that only four people were present. Another training session was added to help prepare for the school workshop, and the final training session took the form of a dress rehearsal. Within two months of the start of the project a format of weekly meetings had been established that was to last for the duration of the project. As Andrew Young remarked in the Ulster Quaker Peace Committee annual report,

> it is pleasing to report that (the field worker) has gathered around him a team of seven or eight voluntary workers who are being trained in the skills needed to work in schools.[12]

In 1989, a volunteer with the German reconciliation organisation Eirene, unhappy with his placement on another project, was recommended to contact QPEP. He stayed with QPEP for the remainder of his placement. This began an informal relationship between QPEP and Eirene that led to five Germans becoming Eirene volunteers with QPEP for at least a year each, between 1989-94. This international link added a welcome dimension and diversity to the team. It was augmented by links with Earlham College in the USA who provided part-time placement students.

Although the team itself went through many changes, and challenges, it was to last the length of the project. A recurring challenge, given the pioneering nature of the work, and conflicting approaches, was how to deal with conflict within the team.

As well as comments in evaluations of training session, a pointer had been made to this key issue inherent in peace education. As previously stated, John Lampen, who was to be an active member of the QPEP team from its inception until its last project, had written that a key quality of peace education is "remaining with conflicts till they are solved."[13] This was to prove a major challenge for the team throughout its existence.

For external agencies, schools, and adult groups, the point of contact for many of them would be the QPEP team of staff and volunteers. Particularly in the context of schools there was a need for sensitivity, the experience of Kingston Friends being especially relevant -

> You must be more professional than the professionals, there is nothing more likely to make a school write off incoming visitors than muddle, lateness or poor planning. Because the discipline is relaxed it is essential that everything runs smoothly: A workshop can fall apart because an activity doesn't work. Nothing can take the place of careful preparation. [14]

For many of the QPEP team, at the start, and for many subsequent members, their own schooling had ended at the earliest opportunity, and was coloured by negative experiences. These were illustrated by separate individual responses to the question about their own childhoods on the first training workshop.

> *What I wished the teacher would never say or do, or hadn't done?*
> Teacher made up a song with a putdown of me in, that the other children had to sing. Teacher picked on me to such an extent that I felt I had to run away from school. Didn't like being singled out or slapped in front of Assembly. Being told off for not holding a wee boy's hand, and being slapped for no reason. Being forced to eat vegetables, and pulled by the hair for watching the girls doing PE. Whole class being slapped because teacher couldn't identify one 'culprit'. [15]

On the same occasion the QPEP team answered the question

> *What qualities did your favourite teacher have?:-*
> Sense of humour, ability to laugh. Look to the child as an individual to communicate with. Where the teacher praised her or coaxed her on. Supported her when it was difficult to understand words. Being remembered, being special. Patience and (had) time for her. Taking time for her, allowing her to do messages. Treated everyone equally and as her equal. Old and

kind and easy going. [16]

In the introduction to the first meeting of the team it was clearly stated that

> the team will aim to be a resource to work alongside teachers, who
> are already having major effect in this area, with their pupils, or
> who are trying to. [17]

As will be discussed later in this report, there was a tension inherent in the work of the QPEP team, who tended to identify with the pupils rather than the teachers, yet who were active in a project whose primary aim was to support teachers who were isolated.

The experience of being in the QPEP team often led to an increase in personal confidence. Writing in the QPEP irregular newsletter, "Dummy Bump", one volunteer made the point that, in addition to the value of the work of the QPEP team it had been important for himself.

> The amount of confidence I have now compared with May is a
> vast improvement. I find it a lot easier to communicate with
> people. [18]

Another volunteer commented,

> the more workshops I do, the clearer I become about what makes
> me react in different ways. [19]

The stamina required to maintain an energy level over a weekly programme at a school represented a considerable commitment from each volunteer. In answer to the question about why they stayed involved, one response was,

> Would it be for the 'crack' of the team, working with teachers, or
> is it the challenge the young people put before me, all the time?[20]

The QPEP team had a considerable changeover in the six years of the project, and later in this report its role in helping define the direction of the Project will be explored.

NOTES

1. Tyrrell, Jerry (1988a) "Formation of a 'Q-PEP TEAM'" - proposal
2. Bowers, Sue et al (1984) "Ways and Means - An Approach to Problem Solving", Kingston Friends Workshop Group.
3. Tyrrell, Jerry (1986) "Nonviolence in the USA", BBC Radio Foyle, February 1986.
4. "QPEP Team Evaluation - Week One; 4th May 1988"
5. Tyrrell, Jerry (1988b) "Week One - what actually happened" report of first workshop, 4th May 1988.
6. "QPEP Team Evaluation - Week Two; 11th May 1988"
7. "QPEP Team Evaluation - Week Three; 18th May 1988"
8. Judson, Stephanie (Ed) (1984) "Manual on Nonviolence and Children" New Society Publishers, Philadelphia Pa, USA.
9. "QPEP Team Evaluation - Week Five; 1st June 1988"
10. Ibid
11. Ibid
12. Ulster Quaker Peace Committee, Ulster Quaker Peace Educatio Project, Report 1987/88, Coleraine.
13. Lampen, John (1987) Kufundisha Amani - A Course in Peace Education for Teachers in Uganda, Institute of Teacher Education, KYAMBOGO, Kampala, Uganda.
14. Bowers, Sue et al (1984)
15. "What I wished the teacher would never say or do, or hadn't done?" QPEP team exercise 4th May 1988.
16. Ibid
17. Tyrrell, Jerry (1988b) Ibid
18. O'Hagan, Paddy (1989) "Dummy Bump No. 1" Quaker Peace Education Project Newsletter, Spring Term 1989.
19. Hannigan, Bridie (1989) "Annual Report 1988/89" Quaker Peace Education Project.
20. Ibid

CHAPTER 3: GETTING INTO SCHOOLS

The July 1985 conference had expressed the view that Quakers were seen as independent and respected as such, and therefore in a position to play an important part in EMU. However in the North West of the province, the Quaker community were few in number, and a relatively unknown quantity. For example, as soon as it became public that the Quaker Peace Education Project was going to be established a primary school teacher contacted me. She was keen to have the QPEP team assist her in the classroom. However, initially this proposal was vetoed by the board of Governors, concerned lest we (QPEP) were engaged in a proselytising exercise.[1]

(Two years later QPEP did a series of workshops with pupils at the school, and subsequently the teacher concerned and I co-led an INSET day for the staff.)

Magee College had no teacher-training role, and although individual teachers enrolled onto MEd programmes, it had few formal links with pre-tertiary education. Members of the Management Committee did however individually have strong links with primary and secondary education in general, and EMU in particular.

As O'Neill pointed out -

> Initially the fieldworker found that he was able to get the best response where people knew him individually, especially through his previous employment.[2]

During the first term at the suggestion of the Management Committee, I made a conscious effort to visit principals of schools, in order to find out what was happening in EMU in Derry.

The invitation that provided the first opportunity for the QPEP team to work with children came from Rosemount Primary School, for a P5/6 class. In subsequent conversations the Principal and the teacher mentioned that they had been aware of the historical role of Quakers in peace education.

On June 10th, less than three months into the life of the Project, the

QPEP team did its first workshop. The objective was to put into practice with children the exercises the team had been preparing for six weeks.

This limited objective belied the significance of the workshop programme in establishing a format and content that was the basis of much of the subsequent development of QPEP's work.

In the first few months of the project, the QPEP team was particularly responding to one of the stated functions of the project of "Identifying and developing untried strategies".[3]

Three key themes of experiential peace education, affirmation, co-operation and communication, were in evidence in the exercises chosen for the first school's workshop. The QPEP team had adapted an exercise from the "Manual of Nonviolence and Children"[4], 'I am lovable and capable'. This explored the effects of putdowns and 'put-ups'. At this first workshop with children, the exercise "Dummy Bump" was created (see page 27).

The workshop benefited from the planning, there was plenty for the children to do, and they enjoyed doing it. It was sufficiently successful for the school to invite the QPEP team back for an eight week programme. Meanwhile I had been negotiating with the Model primary school. As a result a series of weekly workshops was organised with the two schools in parallel. Each week had a theme, and a specific aim built around the theme. For example, for week three the theme was Affirmation, and the aim was

> to identify the things we enjoy doing; that we like about ourselves, the things we care about and are important to us. To share this with others.[5]

The programme would be designed to focus on affirmation activities.

During the course of the series of workshops QPEP was informed that a midweek vacancy had arisen at the Corrymeela Centre in Ballycastle in December. With the agreement of principals of the Model PS, and Rosemount PS, the two classes were booked into the centre. They were to meet for the first time at the centre.

The feedback from both schools, as documented in the 1988/89 annual report, was both positive and realistic about the series of classroom workshops and the residential. Rosemount PS teachers McCabe and Cassidy found it to be an enjoyable learning experience, "the exercises being at once entertaining and fruitful".[6]

They believed that

> teachers and pupils should experience this methodology earlier and for longer periods of time.[7]

McCabe and Cassidy recognised, as other teachers did subsequently, that "observing the pupils at work, the teachers saw a different side to pupils than would be apparent in the normal classroom situation and vice-versa"; the same teachers noticed that the reverse was true, and that the children became aware of a different response of the teachers to these methods, and "a lot more learning took place" as a result.

Nevertheless it wasn't easy. The Rosemount class had a reputation for being hard to handle. The teachers identified one particularly difficult area,

> the volunteers soon realised how easy it was for control to go and found it necessary to adapt quickly to re-establish a receptive atmosphere.[8]

As previously stated this was a inherent danger in the workshop approach. Sue Bowers, co-author of "Ways and Means" [9] which provided the inspiration for many of the activities undertaken at both schools, visited N. Ireland and participated in a workshop with the class at the Model PS. She reflected afterwards on

> what degree of controlled chaos is effective and to whom. Our own workshops are now much more ordered than they were. Bowers She made the point that teachers often find the apparent anarchy stressful.[10]

However the Model PS class teacher writing in the same annual report was at pains to point out that, although he found it difficult to tread the "thin line between teacher and informal adult", the children

> established the difference between the classroom and our work with (the QPEP team) as the team became known, and adapted their attitudes accordingly.[11]

In September 1988, I took over a commitment from John Lampen to teach a sixth form peace studies class at Foyle and Londonderry College on Thursday afternoons. For four of the six years of the project this was to provide a regular weekly opportunity for QPEP staff and volunteers to experience the reality of working with a "mandated" group of young people.

The young people were able to choose "Peace Studies" from a number of options; the compulsory nature of the attendance in the first term was only made explicit when it was clear that of the 17 present only two wanted to be there; the rest would rather have done first-aid or wood-work.

The constraints of attempting a workshop approach in a traditional setting, with a group of reluctant young people made demands on the individuals leading the work. As the young people began to take advantage of the informality of the approach, they were able to address issues and conflicts in their own way, within the clearly established ground rules. In several cases the ten week course led to the young people leading their own workshop on the final afternoon.

The workshops at Foyle and Londonderry College were the only ones that QPEP undertook on their own, without the participation of school staff. Whilst this meant that the young people and QPEP individuals were able to have a direct rapport, it did mean that the work was being done in isolation from the school, even though it was on the school's premises.

Usually the role of the teacher, and the school in general would be the key in the success of every series of workshops. As O'Neill points out,

> There was a variety of responses from teachers to QPEP with regard to their participation in workshops. There were those who wanted QPEP to come in and work with the children but did not

want to be present in the workshops at all. Those who had some experience in lifeskills and/or group work relished the informality of the workshops. Some who had not had such experience were prepared to take part.[12]

In recent years the need for a "whole school approach" has been recognised by people involved in peace education. This involves the whole school community including parents, Governors, and ancillary staff as well as teachers and pupils.

An experienced peace educator talked about her recent experiences in Southern England, at the Mediation UK 1994 conference. She described the different responses she got from schools.

I am working at three schools at the moment and at one school I will go in and they will say, 'Hello, Anne, nice to see you today. Would you like a cup of coffee, the rest of the staff are in there?' I will go into another school and they will say, 'Oh it must be Tuesday, today.' And the other school I go into they look at me as if I have never been there.[13]

Rawlings's experience in England indicates that peace education is not necessarily at the top of any school's priorities. In N. Ireland in 1988, even in the context of supporting teachers working in the field of EMU, this was seen by schools as a peripheral activity since at that time EMU, even as a cross-curricular theme, was not a statutory requirement. Help was sought by QPEP from the Western Education and Library Board.

In the first few months of QPEP's start, the project was anxious to get "a foot in the door", even if its impact would just be on one class. In the first year of the project a number of different approaches were embarked upon to provide support for teachers, to get into schools, and to develop untried strategies.

These approaches included two after-school workshops for secondary school RE teachers, on aspects of reconciliation and conflict, other religious denominations, and prejudice.[14]

As a direct result, QPEP was invited into a secondary school to do work on prejudice reduction, and it also decided to produce a guide to local religious denominations[15]. This was written by the first of five BA Peace Studies undergraduates that QPEP was to have on placement 1989 - 1994.

However it was also clear that the prejudice and conflict resolution module was not a popular choice (in the RE GCSE curriculum). [16]

In May 1988, a number of local teachers and myself participated in a Prejudice Reduction workshop led by Cherie Brown at Corrymeela, Ballycastle. [17] This was to be the first of six annual workshops by Cherie Brown, director of the National Coalition Building Institute, NCBI. The NCBI prejudice reduction process was to figure substantially in the work of QPEP in its work in adult education and secondary schools.

In October 1988, Corrymeela worker Ann Dickson and I led a day workshop using the NCBI model with a group of Quakers, youth workers, cross community workers and teachers.[18]

Subsequently two of the teachers who had been present at both the May and October workshops and I co-led a three day INSET course, for teachers involved in a cross-community scheme, based on the NCBI process.[19]

The report of the workshop written by the tutors indicated that the process was completely new to the teachers, "and led to some resistance from them" on the second day. This was dealt with "sensitively and supportively by the tutors", and "the resulting discussion was .... noted as a high point by several of the participants afterwards." The final day's agenda was changed and

> the previous day's hostility was defused creatively by making the exercises less 'risky' and encouraging participation in a non-threatening way.[20]

This workshop and others using NCBI processes, were helping to fulfil from the outset QPEP's aim of "identifying and developing untried strategies."[21] They also indicated recurring areas of resistance, particularly among teachers, to work which had an emotional context. The challenge of "naturalising" or "acculturising" imported strategies was a major one for QPEP, and its role with NCBI in particular will be explored further in

Chapter 14.

In conjunction with the Workers Educational Association, a local teacher and the fieldworker co-led an evening class entitled "Strategies for Education for Mutual Understanding". In the WEA brochure it was described as a course for "teachers, youth workers, community workers ... involved or interested in EMU". [22] Each of the five fortnightly workshops consisted of a first half of reflecting on past experience of EMU practice, and a second half of skills.

The format of the course allowed people to share the difficulties they experienced with EMU. The isolation, difficulty of finding people to work with from the other community, the need for "teachers and leaders to establish trust and understanding in themselves", illustrated the need for support and training. [23] It was well attended, and led to work being done in a secondary school the following term.

By the Spring Term 1989, QPEP had received invitations to work in St. Brecan's High School, and undertook a series of workshops with fourth formers. Originally intended to be a joint EMU project with local state school, Clondermot, this was not to materialise at that time. The liaison teacher, Gerry Kelly whilst liking the informal relaxed style of the QPEP team, and their presentation, was critical of the lack of preparation and organisation of some sessions. [24]

In March 1989 the QPEP team linked up with Dr Alan Smith at the Centre for the Study of Conflict, for a major EMU project with 3 primary schools in Limavady. The programme of six workshops was based on the work which QPEP had done the previous term with Rosemount PS and the Model PS in Derry. Although not repeated, a successful innovation was the involvement of parents. The whole project was written up as part of the Extending School Links project. [25] Alan Smith wrote a useful summary of the contents and methodology of the six week programme. [26]

Another innovation which was to help QPEP's profile in schools, and establish a tradition, was the "P7 conference". It was John Lampen's idea to acknowledge the value of the ideas of young people of primary school age, and to give them a forum to address issues that concerned them. Inviting delegates from each school to a day conference at an outside venue was a deliberate attempt to give the event a similar status to a 6th form conference. The programme itself was designed for eleven year olds, with a combination of an adult input, games, workshops and an opportunity for the young people themselves to report back. The content of the P7 conferences is described in greater detail in the next chapter.

The significance of the P7 conference in terms of "getting into schools" is that since there was a high turnout from each of the primary schools in the city of Derry at each conference, annually, it helped QPEP 'to get known quickly in all the city's schools and to demonstrate our faith in the children's capacity to transcend differences and work together creatively'.[27]

This was particularly so when the delegates were able to feed back their experience to principals, teachers and their peers. For example, feedback to one principal from children attending the 1993 P7 conference on mediation led to him agreeing to be involved with a pilot peer mediation project.[28]

Within a year of Quaker Peace Education Project starting it had taken a number of initiatives in its efforts to reach and support teachers working in isolation, to identify and develop untried strategies and to arrange skills-training. Although it had not established ongoing groups of like-minded teachers in a formal sense, it was providing support and training for individual teachers.

NOTES

1. Tyrrell, Jerry (1992) "The Ulster Quaker Peace Education Project" in Friends Quarterly, Vol Twenty-Seven No. 2 April 1992.
2. O'Neill, Jim, (1993) "Quaker Peace Education Project Evaluation - Final Report", Charities Evaluation Services, Belfast.
3. "Peace Education in N.I. - New Quaker Initiative", The Friendly Word, March-April 1986.
4. Judson, Stephanie (Ed) (1984) "Manual on Nonviolence and Children" New Society Publishers, Philadelphia Pa, USA.
5. "Proposals for eight week course", Autumn 1988.
6. McCabe, Tommy and Cassidy, John (1989) Annual Report 1988/89, Ulster Quaker Peace Education Project, Derry.
7. Ibid
8. Ibid

9. Bowers, Sue et al (1984) "Ways and Means - An Approach to Problem Solving", Kingston Friends Workshop Group.
10. Bowers, Sue (1989) p43 Annual Report 1988/89, QPEP
11. Harkness, Derek, (1989) p15-18 QPEP Annual Report 1988/89,
12. O'Neill, Jim, (1993) Ibid
13. Rawlings, Anne (1994) Speech at Mediation UK conference, Hayes Conference Centre, Swanwick, 21st June 1994.
14. "Aspects of the GCSE RE syllabus - two linked workshops for teachers, September 1988" - flyer.
15. Lindsay, John (1989) "Different Beliefs - A guide to Churches in Londonderry. QPEP, September 1989
16. "Aspects of the CGSE RE syllabus - two linked workshops for teachers, September 1988" - item in 'Dummy Bump' No 1, Spring Term
17. NICMA. Prejudice Reduction Workshop (1988A) May 27-29 at Corrymeela, Ballycastle, led by Cherie Brown, (NCBI), organised by the Northern Ireland Conflict and Mediation Association.
18. Prejudice Reduction Workshop (1988B) Oct 15th 1988, Magee College,, Derry, led by J Tyrrell and Ann Dickson, Organised by QPEP.
19. Prejudice Reduction Workshop (1988C) Nov 22-24 1988, L'Derry Teacher's Centre, led by Maire Mullan, June Neill and Jerry Tyrrell, Organised by QPEP / Danish Cross Cultural exchange programme.
20. Mullan, Maire; Neill, June and Tyrrell, Jerry (1988) Evaluation of 22-24 Nov. 1988 Prejudice Reduction workshop, Dec 1988.
21. "Peace Education in N.I. - New Quaker Initiative" Ibid.
22. "WEA N. Ireland District Guide to Course - Autumn term 1988",
23. "Difficulties experienced with EMU" (1988), collation of responses, WEA/QPEP evening class, "Strategies for Dealing with EMU", Derry
24. Kelly, Gerry (1989) p21-23 Annual Report 1988/89, QPEP
25. Smith, Alan and Dunn, Seamus (1990), 'Extending Inter-School Links' - University of Ulster, Centre for the Study of Conflict, Coleraine.
26. Smith, Alan (1989), "Myself and Others", A six week programme of education workshops for P7 pupils, leaflet for parents.
27. Lampen, John (1992) ' "Planning Our Future together"
28. Roulston, Michael, (1994) Interviewed by J Tyrrell, 16th June 1994,

CHAPTER 4: INFLUENCES AND INITIATIVES

In July 1988 I attended a conference on Affirmation, Communication, Co-operation, at the Selly Oak colleges in Birmingham Quaker Peace and Service (QPS) were actively involved in organising the conference, and the QPS Education and Advisory Service and QPEP were to keep in close contact throughout QPEP's existence.

At the conference I was able to experience at first hand a workshop by Kingston Friends Workshop Group, and learn the theory behind the methodology of affirmation, communication, co-operation and conflict resolution. This was illustrated by the "Iceberg principle". Conflict is likened to an iceberg, so that when conflict "breaks the surface", you may think you have all of it in view, but the reality is that 90% is below the surface. All too often we try a "quick fix" of the conflict on the surface, forgetting that like an iceberg if we lop off the top conflict, another one will bob to the surface, unless the underlying factors are dealt with. These factors are identified has non co-operation, a lack of communication, and a lack of self-esteem or appreciation; hence the need for affirmation, communication, co-operation as conflict resolution skills; in turn resolving the conflict that has broken the surface.

By 1989 QPEP was using the concept of the iceberg in adult education workshops to illustrate the theory behind what was often perceived as (mere) games. The iceberg demonstrated that there was a thought out methodology behind the affirmation, co-operation or communication exercises.

The 1988 QPS conference also provided the opportunity to learn new exercises and learn new exercises. One in particular, "Red Flags", became a standard exercise in workshops where participants would be encouraged to identify potential situations of conflict.

This cross-fertilisation of ideas was a feature of QPEP. As staff and volunteers experienced new approaches they would be tried out on the next available workshop.

Visits to other projects such as West Midlands Quaker Peace Education Project, and visits by other projects, for example Sue Bowers of Kingston Friends, took advantage of the high quality learning experience afforded by workshops.

In Autumn 1988, I and three volunteers attended the Annual conference of the Forum for Initiatives for Reparation and Mediation (FIRM), at Hoddesdon in Herts. I gave a keynote address, stressing the need in working with children to

> deal with the everyday conflicts in (children's) lives, *before* even beginning to incorporate the added complication of dealing with the 'other tradition'. The relevance of conflict resolution to one of the aims of EMU, that of "learning the importance of resolving difference and conflict by peaceful and creative means."[1]

The conference also provided opportunities for the QPEP team to lead and participate in workshops.

QPEP was beginning to find its niche in the field of experiential peace education.

Dummy Bump

As previously noted, the first school's workshop provided the opportunity for the QPEP team to adapt an existing exercise, (I am Lovable and Capable) to create Dummy Bump.

> Dummy Bump was an (odd looking character) drawn on the blackboard and children (were) encouraged to call out put-downs they heard in the playground. As each one was heard, a bit of DUMMY BUMP was rubbed out until nothing was left of him. Then the class would be asked how to get him back; someone called out, 'Put him in prison'. Sooner or later they realised that calling him positive things would bring him back.[2]

Dummy Bump became a regular feature of children's workshops, and was used to illustrate the effects of putdowns, and start small group discussions. As the work of QPEP became known, this exercise was to inspire feedack and imitation.

We related this story (of Dummy Bump) to a Quaker Conference and the talk about the work of the Project followed a talk about work at the visitor's centre at Maghaberry Prison. The story inspired this poem by the chairperson of the conference Joyce Neill.

Naked and vulnerable we all remain,
Beneath the varied garments we acquire
stitched with experience of joy or pain.

The lucky ones are lapped in love and care,
Warmed with encouragement, dressed in esteem,
Coated in confidence, sure that their lives
are based in reality and not a dream.

But the less fortunate wear different garb:
belittled, non-achieving, unfulfilled
They clothe themselves in violence and resentment;
Thin, useless coverings that leave them chilled.

And then a voice cries loud
from the anonymous crowd;
Send them to prison! [3]

Dummy Bump became a hallmark of the Quaker Peace Education Project. During the visit of Jill Wilsher five years after she had helped facilitate the June 1985 conference, Dummy Bump became a dressed up character. Exercises involving a volunteer dressed as Dummy Bump gave an added edge to the issues of name-calling. It was an exercise that inspired children to explore the effects of bullying.

   In 1994 the exercise was written up by QPEP for "Children working for Peace" an UNICEF publication by the Oxford Development Education Project.[4]   Also in that publication were examples of exercises in, communication and co-operation from other parts of the world.

P7 Conference

The timing of the P7 conference, in the Spring, often coincided with the Peace and Reconciliation Group's "Friendship Week". The P7 Conference was one QPEP activity that had the consistent support of the Western Education and Library Board which provided lunch for the participants through its School Meals Service.

Each year there was a different theme. At the first P7 Conference in May 1989, it was "Your City in the Year 2,000". In a deliberate attempt to acknowledge the value of the contribution of young people to this subject, Derry's Guildhall was chosen as a venue. The format was a series of ice-breaker games followed by a five minute input from each of four visiting adult experts. Topics included leisure, the environment, employment and security. Workshops led by QPEP members and the "experts" allowed the children to explore these topics. After lunch the children re-grouped into different groups and prepared their submissions about the sort of city they wanted to live in. The day culminated in a press conference.

This format of standard QPEP activities such as ice-breakers, the involvement of outside agencies or individuals with specialised knowledge or expertise, focussed workshops for the children, and a creative opportunity to express the outcome, was repeated each year.

In 1990 the theme was "Friends and Rivals" and focussed on gender. A drama tutor and students from Stranmillis College set up a dramatic situation for the morning session. In the afternoon the QPEP team took over, and the children had to answer questions about what was good about being a boy or a girl, and discussed what had been written. As a result of the day a Children's Charter was produced.

The 1991 theme was "Imagining a World without Weapons". For this the QPEP team devised a new exercise whereby each child "was asked what animal she or he would like to be; and then the groups worked out how to create a zoo for themselves."[5]

This was a complicated exercise, as it required thinking about issues of safety and freedom. The day's programme continued, with factual topics such as "war and the environment"; "guns and crime" and the "arms race". Each topic group was led by an adult with a particular speciality in the field.

The outcome of the day was a huge wall newspaper "the New World", dated five years hence.

> It covered a wide range of subjects from serious articles expressing the longing for peace in Ulster, and humorous variants ... to adverts for toys ('Peace Action Man').[6]

The annual P7 Conference was a challenge to QPEP not least because it required a fresh approach each year.

Ground Rules

An essential part of the workshop process was creating a co-operative environment. During its first workshops the Quaker Peace Education Project developed four ground rules. These were "No Putdowns", "One Person Speaking At A Time", "Confidentiality" and "You May Pass".

QPEP was working with classes of children who were used to raising their hands in response to a question. Often this was the only constraint to stop them speaking all at once. To aid the implementation of this ground rule, the QPEP team borrowed the idea of a "Quiet Please" sign from "Ways and Means".[7] In time this became a "lollipop" sign with Quiet Please on one side and Thank You on the other.

In 1990 I attended a workshop run by facilitators of the Alternatives to Violence Programme (AVP), and as a result introduced their two additional ground rules - "Look for and point out positive qualities in one another", and "Volunteer yourself only".

Each of the now six ground rules had a rationale which was designed to create the safety necessary for people to take risks and deal with conflicts.

The "no putdown" rule in particular was hard to enforce, some participants felt that this would lead to a lack of banter or "craic", which in turn would make the experience dull. Significantly the opposite was usually the case, workshops were fun and a hallmark of workshops was the laughter. Overhearing the laughter at the end of a QPEP workshop, a passing facilitator was intrigued as his particular field was the use of humour in resolving conflict.[8]

The debate about the relative merits of the "no putdown" rule, affirmation, and criticism in terms of the honest debate deemed necessary to resolve conflict was to form the basis of a series of articles in the Community Relations Journal at the end of the project.[9]

In the first phase of the Quaker Peace Education Project the workshop format was used to disseminate the experience of the QPEP team at conferences and seminars. QPEP began to have an occasional input into the MA Peace Studies course, using this experiential approach in contrast to the traditional lecture.

Networking with groups broadly involved in peace education in N. Ireland, the Irish Republic, Britain and further afield also ensure cross-fertilisation of ideas as well keeping the QPEP team abreast of the latest developments in the field.

NOTES

1. Tyrrell, Jerry (1988) "Developments in conflict resolution in schools in Northern Ireland", Forum for Initiatives in Reparation and Mediation (FIRM) annual conference, Hoddesdon, Herts, 31st October 1988.
2. "Dummy Bump", Article in "Dummy Bump" occasional newsletter of QPEP, Issue No. 2; Easter 1990.
3. Ibid
4. "Children working for Peace" (1994) Second draft by UNICEF and the Oxford Development Education Centre.
5. Lampen, John (1992) ' "Planning Our Future together" A project from Northern Ireland describes a series of primary school conferences which might inspire similar work elsewhere'.
6. Ibid.
7. Bowers, Sue et al (1984) "Ways and Means - An Approach to Problem Solving", Kingston Friends Workshop Group.
8. The sixteenth congress of the International Society for Intercultural Education Training and Research (SIETAR), Kilkenny 7 - 12th April 1990.
9. Issues 5, 6, 7; Quarterly Journal for Community Relations Trainers and Practitioners, Community Relations Council, Belfast.

CHAPTER 5: ACTION RESEARCH

Within six months of its inception QPEP had found a niche for itself within the UK peace education field. Previous chapters have illustrated that QPEP fitted into an experiential Peace Education tradition that included the Nonviolence and Children Committee in Philadelphia, Creative Responses to Conflict, and Kingston Friends Workshop Group. The manuals of each of these agencies influenced the thinking and activities of the QPEP team. In these manuals, evaluation was given a key role in the process of improving practice, and this process provides a form of action research.

For example, the Manual on Nonviolence and Children[1], quotes a format of evaluation, which can be done individually or by a group. Three columns of flipchart or A4 paper are headed:

+	-	
Things that were good	Things that weren't good and/or need changing	Ways to Improve or things to keep in mind.

For the initial QPEP team training workshops, this was used by the team members at the end of each morning. They provided useful pointers for areas that needed covered the following week. As a general rule, workshops' participants would be invited to fill in such sheets after each workshop. (Later QPEP staff and volunteers would experience "Alternatives to Violence Project" (AVP) which used 'running evaluations', within its workshops).

"Ways and Means" [2] provided a useful rationale for this type of evaluation,

> It encourages critical judgment; it shows the workshop team which activities are popular and/or useful and suggests possible amendments; it encourages a feeling of participation and the belief, particularly valuable to those lacking in self-respect, that their opinions are sought and valued; it develops the ability to

assess personal performance, not compared with other people but against their own potential. This leads to better self-knowledge in other fields - 'Why am I angry/hurt/afraid?' It allows people to practise expressing criticism in a positive, non-threatening way.[3]

The balance between affirmation and criticism became an issue within the QPEP team. Bowers argues that

some groups never get as far as self-evaluation, people who receive little or no personal affirmation are only too aware of their shortcomings, of which they are constantly reminded. Help in recognising their achievements is what they need above all.[4]

A classic example of this was half-way through the first series of workshops at Rosemount Primary School. After one particularly rowdy workshop, when it seemed the children were unable to keep even the most basic ground rule of one person speaking at a time, leading to facilitators shouting, and generally undermining the basic aims of the workshop, the team met to evaluate the workshop. Feelings of failure overwhelmed the team, and in a desperate attempt to save the situation, the team affirmed each member in turn. This provided the energy to look on the workshop as a learning experience, and to identify the areas for improvement.

The challenge for the QPEP team generally was to develop members self-confidence to a point where people could be honest about themselves and know they would be understood.

Implicit in evaluation is the need to link the outcome to the aim; and although in the early days of the project the aims of every workshop were made explicit as part of the programme, this practise lapsed. This naturally created dissatisfaction amongst the volunteers. Towards the end of the project the practice of linking the participant's evaluation forms to the expressed aims of the particular workshop was introduced, helping to improve the quality of the feedback.

Prutzman makes the point that "suggestions (arising from evaluation) should be followed up as quickly as possible".[5] Another recurring criticism from volunteers was that mistakes made on one workshop, or series of workshops were being repeated; and where evaluations had taken place they weren't necessarily being read prior to the planning of a similar subsequent series of workshops.

Elliott defines action-research as "the study of a social situation with a view to improving the quality of action within it".[6] Throughout the life of QPEP it was the volunteers in the QPEP team as much as the staff who strived to ensure that the "quality of the action" was improved, by incorporating the results of the research.

The CES evaluation[7] was to indicate the shortcomings of the research side of the project. The first requests for QPEP to do workshops were accepted almost automatically. Each workshop became an opportunity for the QPEP team to try out its approaches, and adapt new exercises.

Very quickly the project began to be "workshop" driven; the energy of the staff and volunteer team was focussed on the "action". Through sheer force of numbers decisions had to be taken about which workshop should be accepted. Planning the *research* side of the project tended to be in terms of individual workshops. Although the Management Committee consistently urged me to write up the project, and publish results, it was difficult to restrict the programme to the optimum number of workshops necessary to create time for adequate reflection and writing.

Early on in the life of QPEP it became clear that the hour or two of the actual workshop was only a fraction of the time commitment that was required from the QPEP team. To the regular weekly planning morning was added the time for evaluation of individual workshops.

Although its "action" role became defined early on, defining QPEP's research role within the University as a project of the Centre for the Study of Conflict took longer. As mentioned in Chapter 3, QPEP had a substantial input into Alan Smith's research related to his "Extending School Links" project.[8]

More substantial research was undertaken through contact with the Peace and Conflict Studies courses at the University of Ulster.

As well as representation on the Management Committee its links with the Peace Studies courses were strengthened by my enrolling on the MA Peace Studies Course. In particular the discipline of carrying out a detailed evaluation of the Peace Education work I did in Uganda brought me into direct contact with action research processes.[9] The course tutor commented that:

> this assignment illustrates the supportive function of part-time study in Peace Education for on-going professional work. The exercise has clearly furthered the quality of that work for the assignment promoted planning, organisation and the attention to detail.[10]

It linked the evaluation with the expressed aims of the stakeholders, and provided an analysis of the changes needed to transfer Western exercises into a Ugandan context.

For five of the six years of the project, QPEP had a third year Peace and Conflict Studies student on placement from January to June. As well as playing an active part in facilitating workshops, each student did significant research work. (See Appendix 1).

The first major piece of research of QPEP's work was carried out by placement student Marian McClintock during her placement in 1990.

As well as documenting two days of workshops, it provided a broader overview as to whether the aims of the project were being met. McClintock answered this question in the affirmative, adding that "as the project has developed, new goals and ambitions are also being achieved." [11]

This research attempted to link the theory of prejudice to the NCBI model, and came to the conclusion that although the model was not flawed in its own right, in the context of EMU it may be "necessary for QPEP and teachers to take a closer look at the school's curriculum and modify the model to suit their needs."[12]

In 1991, I completed my MA with a dissertation exploring reasons for resistance by teachers to the NCBI processes. [13]

By 1990 QPEP was being referred to as an action-research project, and a seminar was convened at the Centre for the Study of Conflict at the my request. My dissertation "itself afforded an opportunity to explore current thinking about action-research within the Centre (for the Study of Conflict)."[14]

NOTES

1. Judson, Stephanie (Ed) (1984) "Manual on Nonviolence and Children" New Society Publishers, Philadelphia Pa, USA.
2. Bowers, Sue et al (1984) "Ways and Means - An Approach to Problem Solving", Kingston Friends Workshop Group.
3. Ibid
4. Ibid
5. Prutzman et al, (1977) "The Friendly Classroom for a Small Planet" Quaker Project on Community Conflict, New York NY.
6. Elliott, J (1982) "Action-research: A framework for self-evaluation in schools. Working paper No. 1. Teacher-Pupil interaction and the Quality of Learning", London Schools Council, mimeo.
7. O'Neill, Jim (1993) Quaker Peace Education Project Evaluation - Final Report", Charities Evaluation Services, Northern Ireland Regional Centre, Belfast.
8. Smith, Alan and Dunn, Seamus (1990) 'Extending Inter-School Links' - An evaluation of contacts between Protestant and Catholic pupils in N. Ireland, University of Ulster, Centre for the Study of Conflict, Coleraine.
9. Tyrrell, Jerry (1989) "Peace Education: An Evaluation of a Short Course for Teachers and Teacher-Trainers in Uganda". Unit F, MA in Peace Studies, University of Ulster, Magee.
10. Robinson, (1989) Comments on Tyrrell, Jerry (1989) "Peace Education:
11. McClintock, Marian (1991) "The Workshop Approach to Prejudice Reduction. BA Thesis.
12. Ibid.
13. Tyrrell, Jerry (1991) "The NCBI Prejudice Reduction Model - Teachers' Resistance in N. Ireland" MA Peace Studies, Magee College, University of Ulster, dissertation.
14. Ibid

CHAPTER 6: INTERNATIONAL WORK
INTERNATIONAL WORK: UGANDA

Prior to the establishment of QPEP, John Lampen had spent two periods in Uganda developing a manual of Peace Education, "Kufundisha Amani".[1] This contact had been developed through Quaker Peace and Service in London, and in 1989 John Lampen encouraged me to take on the follow-up visit. I co-led a peace education course for teachers, at the Church of Uganda training and conference centre in Kampala.

It provided an opportunity to "filter" or fine tune exercises that had been tried and tested in N. Ireland, into a different culture. I would demonstrate the exercise to my co-trainer, and in the process of explanation would adapt it, prior to leading the exercise with the participants.

One classic example of the involvement of the participants in adapting an exercise incorporated the Kingston Friends Workshop Group conflict resolution model of an iceberg.

> Conscious that the properties of icebergs would not be as well known in Uganda as they were in Britain, I asked the participants for a suitable alternative. The essence of the image was that it had 10% 'above the surface'. Immediately I was given the example of the hippopotamus which lies in the water with only its eyes and nose visible.[2]

The Ugandan trainers had a background in the "Training for Transformation" model.[3] This model was based on a number of sources including Paulo Freire, but its main influence on the course was that it provided a context of experiential adult education. The discipline of ensuring that QPEP exercises fitted in with the objectives of the course, and were culturally specific, was a more explicit example of a process that is required at every workshop.

This already strong link with Uganda was consolidated two years later when one of the Ugandan trainers, Rev Onono-Onweng visited QPEP. He used his visit to strengthen his campaign for Peace Education in Uganda.[4]

INTERNATIONAL WORK: FORMER SOVIET UNION

Other international developments in the first three years of the Quaker Peace Education Project included establishing links with the then Soviet Union. In January 1991, QPEP was asked by Quaker Peace and Service (QPS) to put on a workshop for a group of Soviet Visitors. The QPEP team "felt we could only agree if it was a genuine event for the children".[5] There was also some concern about the presence of a large number of adults at a children's workshop.

The elegant solution was to bring together a dozen children from each of two schools for a full workshop, and to involve the visiting adults in an introductory and closing exercise. The adults spent the intervening period watching the workshop on closed circuit television.

Subsequently John Lampen joined a QPS group paying a return visit to North Ossetia, whose task was to "introduce our approach to peace education in an area of simmering ethnic tensions".[6]

QPEP's previous experience in Uganda was a help in preparing a course. The January experience of doing a "Demonstration" workshop for adults formed a model for the work in North Ossetia, only this time the teachers were present in the room and the workshop was presented in a "fishbowl" process. The teachers subsequently had an opportunity to lead the exercises themselves. The course provided

> new experiences and new understandings .... that individual feelings mattered, that it is possible to work without strict hierarchy, and that learning can be fun.[7]

The visit was to be the start of an ongoing contact built up between John Lampen and various agencies in the former Soviet Union.

INTERNATIONAL WORK: UNITED STATES OF AMERICA

In Chapter 14, QPEP's use of National Coalition Building Institute (NCBI) models in line with its original aim of "identifying and developing untried strategies" is documented. In April 1990 I had the opportunity of participating in a series of meetings and assisting leading a three day workshop at the then headquarters of NCBI in Boston, MA, USA. This enabled me to assess the impact of familiar processes in a more ethnically diverse culture, and to work as part of a similarly diverse team of leaders.

QPEP was beginning to become aware that the work of NCBI was more than developing untried strategies, and "not just about participating in workshops but leading them, and not just about workshops but leadership generally".[8]

For a brief period in 1990, QPEP became directly involved in the US based "Peace in Ireland" project. I met one of its members in Boston in April, and as a result she and three other representatives participated in a QPEP prejudice reduction workshop at Blackrock, Co Dublin in August. Five of the participants in that workshop, including members of the QPEP team and a local teacher, were then invited to participate in the "Forum" in Providence, Rhode Island in November. As part of this visit, some of the group made a presentation about the work of QPEP, in Boston. This included a video of a children's workshop, especially filmed for the purpose, which was also shown on Cable TV. At the presentation, people in the audience were amazed that conflict resolution skills workshops were taking place with children in N. Ireland, and even more surprised to discover that the US had provided a lot of the inspiration for the original exercises.

QPEP took advantage of international opportunities in Ireland. A team of three people led workshops at the SIETAR conference in Kilkenny in April 1990, one of which used the NCBI process. The team was apprehensive about working with the participants many of whom had an academic background, as they were inexperienced in working in that environment. Nevertheless the feedback from two of the professors in particular indicated that the workshop had a significant impact on them [9,10]

European Network for Conflict Resolution in Education (ENCORE)

In October 1990 the Quaker Council for European Affairs organised a seminar in Brussels to discuss the setting up of a European Network on Conflict Resolution. This seminar of practitioners from Belgium, England, Germany and Ireland was largely inspired by Jamie Walker's report "Violence and Conflict Resolution in Schools" [11]. The programme which was facilitated by the participants in turn, enabled visions to be shared, as well as concepts, methods and problems associated with the participant's work in the field of education. There were 12 people present, of whom 8 or 9 were English. A report of the seminar identified some key issues that faced practitioners, such as putting lessons in a form that 6 or 7 year olds could understand; convincing teachers that "this work is worthwhile and not peripheral"; coping when the style of discipline in school undermines our own; dealing with hopelessness; introducing mediation to be the key form of discipline; coping with lack of indigenous leadership.[12]

At this seminar it was decided to form a network, to encourage and support the development of conflict resolution work in other countries; to organise seminars and summer schools, and generally to promote the work. The name ENCORE (European Network of Conflict Resolution in Education) was agreed, and in 1991 a more representative group met.

NOTES

1. Lampen, John (1987) Kufundisha Amani - A Course in Peace Education for Teachers in Uganda, Kampala, Uganda.
2. Tyrrell, Jerry (1990a) p21 "Hippopotami and Icebergs", Annual Report 1989/90, Ulster Quaker Peace Education Project.
3. Hope, Anne & Timmel, Sally (1989) "Training for Transformation - A Handbook for Community workers" - Mambo Press, Zimbabwe.
4. Onono-Onweng, Rev Nelson (1991) p2 "Report of a visit to QPEP 5-12 May 1991", Annual Report 1990/91, QPEP, Derry.
5. Lampen, John (1991) "QPEP reaches the Caucuses", Annual Report 1990/91, Ulster Quaker Peace Education Project, Derry.
6. Ibid
7. Ibid.
8. Tyrrell, Jerry (1990b) p28 "Teaparty in Boston - USA", Annual Report 1989/90, Ulster Quaker Peace Education Project.
9. Dungey, Bob (1990) p27 "Report of QPEP workshop at SIETAR , Kilkenny, April 1990", Annual Report 1989/90, QPEP, Derry.
10.Tyrrell, Jerry (1993) p7 Annual Report 1992/93,QPEP
11.Walker, Jamie (1989) "Violence and Conflict Resolution in Schools", Council for Cultural Co-Operation. Council of Europe, Strasbourg.
12. Bentley, Marigold (1990) "Conflict Resolution/Mediation Seminar, QCEA Brussels 5-7 Oct 1990"

CHAPTER 7: ADULT EDUCATION WORK

At the July 1985 conference it was anticipated that QPEP would perform a number of functions, including arranging the provision of skills-training for peace-educators; providing a measure of feedback to established and developing ventures; and liaising with other groups developing peace education.

These functions were not tied to work in schools, and so allowed QPEP to develop work in the youth service, and with adult groups, whether or not the latter included teachers. It has already been mentioned that QPEP readily liased with groups in Britain and further afield. The workshop approach lent itself to the more informal, experiential approach associated with adult education.

In the first three years of the project partnerships were established with groups like Co-Operation North and Protestant and Catholic Encounter (PACE). In April 1989, QPEP was asked to lead a conflict resolution session as part of a training weekend for a group of youth workers from both sides of the border organised by Co-Operation North.

> Three members of the QPEP team arrived in Navan, late on a Saturday night, to lead a Sunday morning workshop on "Conflict Resolution". (The Co-Operation North leader) talked about the participants, who happened to include a nun, a member of the Garda Siochanna, a disabled person, (and) a member of the travelling community, so the QPEP team decided to change the format of the workshop, to deal with prejudice, instead.[1]

The value of the adaptation of the programme to fit the needs of the group was recognised by the Co-Operation North leader,

> Through highlighting particular prejudices by raising the issue of travelling people, some participants for the first time acknowledged that prejudices do exist within their own personality. This session on prejudice reduction was not only successful but also vital in that the participants themselves can bring some of this

experience to bear on the programming of their own youth links exchange.[2]

That particular session began a partnership between QPEP and Co-Operation North which explored ways of incorporating a prejudice reduction element in all their youth and schools exchanges.

This partnership formed the basis of Co-Operation North's own successful "Ourselves and Others" Programme which involves freelance facilitators delivering a prejudice reduction session on weekend exchanges.[3]

Often one workshop would lead to another; an example of this was when the field officer of PACE attended a prejudice reduction workshop led by the QPEP team at the biennial Corrymeela Summerfest in July 1989. Writing in the PACE Journal in 1992, he acknowledged the impact of QPEP's work.

> Their work raised my self-awareness about the role of emotion in group activity. I began to see how important it was to create the right conditions if difficult personal experiences were to be shared. I have involved myself in several 'QPEP weekends' since then, and I have also arranged for QPEP to take weekends for PACE members. Their work has helped some PACE groups to become more activity-based in the approach to anti-sectarian work.[4]

QPEP's endeavours to assist McKittrick in activating PACE groups in this direction using experiential work were not without problems. McKittrick was aware that "the work of mutual understanding which PACE undertakes, is not a soft option". Through its work in co-operation with PACE, QPEP was able to experience working with a significant number of individuals who had been active with PACE for twenty years or more. At one AGM, individuals were dismissive of workshop exercises, saying "This may be all right for children, but we're too old for all that".[5]

It was clear that it was necessary to make gradual changes to the format of institutions, and an Annual General Meeting was not necessarily the right place to introduce an inter-active element. Where adequate advance notice was given, and workshops took place at a more informal setting, such as a regular PACE group meeting, the response from participants was more favourable.

QPEP's association with these two agencies was mutually beneficial, and in each case illustrated that QPEP, co-operating with a sympathetic individual within an agency with similar aims could assist that person in making significant changes.

As previously mentioned, QPEP created a relationship with the Workers Educational Association early in the life of the Project. Although three separate courses ran for a term each, subsequent attempts to run conflict resolution or prejudice reduction courses for the WEA were unsuccessful due to poor turnout.

Throughout its existence QPEP was invited to give inputs into one-off workshops in N. Ireland and the Irish Republic. In the first phase of the project these included groups as diverse as the staff of a children's home; staff and volunteers of cross community contact schemes; youth groups in N. Ireland and the Irish Republic and a children's campaigning organisation (Playboard) .

The themes of the workshops varied from "Handling aggression", and "What is Peace", to "Breaking out of Cultural Stereotypes" and "Dealing with Sectarianism". The programme in each case was based on conflict resolution skills, or prejudice reduction work, and tailored to fit the needs of the particular agency.

Through its University connections, QPEP started to have an irregular input into the Peace and Conflict Studies BA and MA courses. It also developed links with the School for International Training which organised study tours for US students.

Workshops with student groups provided an opportunity for QPEP to share, and receive feedback about, the latest developments in its approaches.

A criticism of QPEP in working with existing reconciliation or peace agencies was that it was "preaching to the converted". The implication was that this was a soft option. For a number of reasons, (apart from the fact that it was a stated aim of the project) working with such groups assisted the development of QPEP.

In 1989 Gerry Kennedy became the first employee of the Peace and Reconciliation Group, in Derry, to become a volunteer with QPEP. This established a working relationship that was to be maintained for the greater part of the life of QPEP.

QPEP was an *experiential* project, it was trying out new and untried strategies, particularly with its NCBI work, and it made sense to start in a "safe" environment, where mistakes could be made and learnt from. Individual exercises could be tried out with adult groups who would often provide the feedback necessary for refinement and who would have the patience to allow for it.

It could be said that the individuals who made up the group at any workshop were on a continuum which ranged from being resistant to exercises at one end, to a willingness to "lap it up" at the other. Individuals aren't static. They might move from one end of the continuum to the other. Workshops go through several stages. Initial activities deal with nervousness, resistance and uncomfortableness. The identification of hopes, fears and expectations and the creation of a co-operative atmosphere. As the group feels more comfortable it is more prepared to tackle controversial issues, and look at difficult feelings. A workshop would often end with an affirmation activity, where individuals shared what they appreciated about the experience, and about each other.

In trying out challenging material, it made sense therefore to work with groups who were present of their own volition, were as fully aware as possible of the nature of the experience and had a positive attitude towards it. This couldn't be guaranteed with any group. Preaching to the converted was something of a misnomer; in N. Ireland "the converted" is often a code for people who are already committed to bringing protestant and catholic together. But it is often presumed in such circles that they themselves are free of prejudice.

It was therefore an uncomfortable experience for some individuals to be faced with the realisation, during the course of prejudice reduction workshops, that there were often consistent outgroups, (for example smokers, feminists, gay/lesbians and travellers). Towards whom the 'converted' held prejudical attitudes even though they were present in their group.

This recurring experience illustrates that the process of "conversion" is a life-long one, and that part of the process of prejudice reduction is acknowledgment that we each have prejudices we are not yet aware of. Another benefit about working with similar agencies was that this also assisted in leadership development. QPEP was consistent throughout its life in encouraging individuals to take on leadership. This was out of self interest as far as the project was concerned, the more leaders there were, the more the leadership was shared.

Repeated participation in workshops has limited value in terms of the individual's development. However, as a leader - taking a greater responsibility with each workshop - his or her confidence and competence grows in leaps and bounds.

From time to time QPEP was to have the opportunity of working with a group or agency which, at first sight, might fall outside the parameters of the project. As a result it was necessary to consult with the management committee.

One such opening arose through the work of the Ulster Quaker Service Committee. I spoke at a Quaker conference in Dublin, and the preceding speaker, Marty Rafferty, spoke about her work for UQSC at the Visitors Centre at HMP Maghaberry. I was aware that a number of conflict resolution skills projects in the USA which worked in formal education, also ran workshops in prisons.

With the Management Committee's agreement I co-led a series of workshops at HMP Maghaberry. I was

> keen to discover whether the exercises we undertook to develop skills in children, young people and adults outside are relevant to (prisoners).[6]

My co-facilitator was Joan Broder (on secondment from Extern to the Probation Dept), and the two of us had two lengthy planning sessions. The prison work was written up in two short articles in the 1989/90 annual report.[7]

Throughout the planning the we ensured that the programme fitted in with the life-prisoners' agenda. This had been clearly stated at a preparatory meeting as being about the issues facing prisoners as a consequence of visits from their families. Consequently there was no inclusion in the original programme of any reference to sectarian issues.

I had previously attended workshops facilitated by leaders of the

"Alternatives to Violence Project" (AVP) which was generated out of work in US prisons, and which relied on affirmation, communication and appreciation exercises. It also was based on a concept of a "Transforming Power" which inspired nonviolent choices in violent situations. At the time of these workshops I did not have enough experience of either AVP or work in prisons, to have the confidence to start using AVP concepts like "Transforming Power".

The experience of working in prison, with men who had experienced life-threatening situations, reinforced for me the validity of processes that could be universally applied in terms of conflict resolution, such as affirmation, co-operation and communication.

NOTES

1. White, Ian (1989) p41 "Co-Operation North", Annual Report 1988/89, Ulster Quaker Peace Education Project, Derry.
2. Ibid.
3. Co-Operation North (1991) "Ourselves and Others - Facilitator Procedure manual" Co-Operation North, Belfast and Dublin.
4. McKittrick, David (1992) p35 "PACE - A Field Officer's Perspective", PACE Volume 24 No. 1.
5. Anonymous, (1989) Comment at QPEP workshop at Protestant and Catholic Encounter (PACE) AGM 28.10.89, Belfast.
6. Tyrrell, Jerry (1990) p34 "Conflict Resolution workshops in Prison", Annual Report 1989/90, Ulster Quaker Peace Education Project, Derry.
7. Ibid

CHAPTER 8: SEEDS OF RESISTANCE

'That's all very well but what about the real world!' (Teacher, Hampton workshop 1990)

Previous chapters hinted at tensions between QPEP, with its informal team of staff and volunteers, and teachers with a more formal approach to education.

Individual members of the QPEP team were ambivalent too, about working with teachers as their peers, when their last experience of schooling had often been negative. In the first phase of the project it became apparent that whereas pupils generally looked forward to workshops with the QPEP team, teachers were ambivalent.

The general appearance of the QPEP team illustrated the difference between it and teachers.

> Their (the QPEP team) dress and manner was generally less conservative than the rest of the group (of researchers, parents and teachers), and this helped them identify closely with the pupils, perhaps encouraging children to see them more as a friend... than an adult in a teaching role.[1]

The physical structure of the workshop encouraged equal participation; and for a teacher this meant physically sitting as an equal to a pupil. This lack of visible hierarchical status could be offputting to the teacher - particularly when s/he had allowed an outsider to be in charge of the proceedings. QPEP discovered that some teachers faced with a situation where the chairs have been set up in a circle would sometimes decide to sit *outside* the circle.

Participation in the circle, as an equal with the pupils, carried its own dilemmas for the teacher. Smith and Dunn point out:-

> Volunteers encouraged children to use first name terms, though teachers were less comfortable with this approach having to reconcile it with the more formal terms of address used back in school.[2]

In practice this usually became relevant at the start of a workshop, where the participants were expected to write their name on a label which they stuck to their clothes. The issue of 'first name or not' was resolved by each individual adult writing the name s/he wanted to be known by. Some teachers would write 'Mr', 'Mrs', or 'Miss'. Others wrote their first names, and found the children, initially at least, hesitant to use them.

Smith and Dunn acknowledged that this gave rise to discussion within the group, particularly around the "level of formalism required to be effective".

Nevertheless Smith and Dunn concluded that

> the emergence of these issues considerably enhanced the experience of the organising group and, rather than generating tension, encouraged issues to be discussed openly.[3]

As the project developed it was not always the case that such issues were discussed openly, and the "dress and manner", youth, and nonteaching nature of the QPEP team, were sometimes barriers to their being "allowed in" to work with the teaching profession.

> In relation to professionalism it was pointed out that teachers on in-service courses often expect to be instructed by others who come from a teaching background. Many of the volunteers in QPEP were young and often casually dressed. This has tended to put some of the teachers off.[4]

Even towards the end of the project, a teacher was to remark in the context of how members of the team were dressed that

> I wondered how I could introduce (them) in the school, and at the same time maintain the seriousness of the 11+. As it turned out (the team) proved very professional; that became clear even before they came to the children. From the first planning session it became clear that these were very committed people and any initial reservations I had ... as the saying goes, 'Don't judge a book

by the cover'.[5]

Likewise there was a need for the QPEP team not to stereotype teachers, or to undervalue the significant work that teachers were doing using a more traditional approach.

McCartney quotes a policy statement from the Northern Ireland Council for Education Development ,

> Any initiatives or increased exhortations of schools to strengthen commitment to education for understanding must not be presented in such a way as to imply a lack of esteem for their current work.[6]

Lampen writing in the 1989/90 QPEP Annual Report made the point that,

> The Project has been welcomed by teachers. But is this because they enjoy a break from the usual timetable, and a chance to relax while a young and lively set of visitors takes over in the classroom? ... An important aim of the Project is to teach the skills for education for mutual understanding. So we need to ask ourselves whether our teamwork approach, the emphasis on learning through games, and the way we establish our working relationship with children are too different from the work-style of most teachers.[7]

There is no doubt that teachers had to adjust to QPEP's interactive approach. A key constraint on teachers was the potentially threatening nature of the informality of the workshop. Smith and Dunn recognise this when they state,

> teachers, as well as pupils, are being asked to find new forms of working together and this inevitably draws them away from their traditional experience of working alone with a class in the confines of a classroom.[8]

Weissglass makes a similar point in a North American context:-

> Mandating educational change is the antithesis of empowerment. It sends a message to teachers that they are inadequate and unappreciated for their efforts and that people outside schools, often people who are rarely in classrooms, are the experts with the answers. It leads to teachers feeling bad about themselves and creates resistance to their thinking through issues for themselves.[9]

Herein lies one of the constraints for teachers taking on board new ideas, and new ways of working. If teachers feel unappreciated, 'put upon', and faced with additional responsibilities, - and undoubtedly this is an effect of the demands of the Northern Ireland Curriculum - then stress rather than self-esteem is likely to be the result.

A lack of self-esteem in teachers themselves is clearly one constraint on the ability of the individual teacher to encourage self-esteem in children. Another constraint is that we live in a put-down culture; sarcasm is often used to put children 'in their place'. Arguably this is even more so since corporal punishment was banned in the mid 1980's.

At a QPEP workshop with primary school children in a rural area of N. Ireland in 1989, a problem solving exercise was in progress. The children had been asked to participate in a 'brainstorming' activity. Brainstorming is designed to generate a multiplicity of solutions, the validity of an individual response being secondary to the aim of triggering off unlikely solutions, or original answers that might break an impasse. No comments are allowed during the process. Despite this, one pupil's suggestion was immediately responded to by a teacher who said, 'Don't you think you're too old to need that?'. The statement was inappropriate for two reasons; firstly it was a comment in an exercise which was meant to be without comment. Secondly, the tone of the comment could be taken as being dismissive of the idea, and consequently a putdown of the child.

This example illustrates the need for teachers as well as pupils to adapt to a new vocabulary, as well as abiding by the ground rules, one of which is 'No Put Downs', another one being 'Look for and affirm positive qualities in one another'.

Bowers stresses the importance of the role of outsiders in not undermining the teacher's position,

Whilst many teachers welcome outsiders others may feel threatened by visitors who bring popular activities into the schoolroom, and a workshop has failed badly if it has made the teacher's job more difficult.[10]

Bowers reinforces the need for support for teachers:-

It is absolutely vital that the workshop team show complete loyalty to the regular teachers; not the blind pretence that all is perfect, but an attempt to explore honestly the underlying causes of difficult situations.[11]

Specifically in a Northern Ireland context, Smith and Dunn conclude that:-

Work of this type (eg Inter School Links) cannot avoid raising issues for teachers which involves them in re-examining their own emotions and feelings about the 'other community' in Northern Ireland.[12]

In his appropriately titled 'Teachers Have Feeling: What Can We Do About It' Weissglass quotes Maria Montessori

... nothing is more difficult for a teacher than to give up her old habits and prejudices. He continues with Fullan in 'The Meaning of Educational Change', change is a difficult, personal, and social process of unlearning old ways and learning new ones.[13]

Weissglass argues that teachers need support in order to deal with emotions - and Smith and Dunn have identified that emotions are inevitable on Inter School Links. Weissglass maintains that structures are needed to enable:-

Educators to look at emotional issues in a constructive manner rather than: (i) avoiding them (which can foster passivity and create resentment); (ii) lecturing about them (which can create boredom); or (iii) dealing with them haphazardly (which can result in people being disruptive or feeling neglected).[14]

By the end of the first phase of the project in 1991, QPEP was becoming aware of the work it needed to do with teachers, in order to overcome resistance. Pearse McGranaghan, a student on placement with the project was uneasy about the way in which QPEP seemed to be seeing "teachers as aliens to our work, instead of seeking to make them allies",[15] in effect stereotyping them.

He organised a seminar with the QPEP team of staff and volunteers which brought his concerns to their attention. The second phase of the project was to concentrate more on working *alongside* teachers.

Considering the major changes involved in implementing Education for Mutual Understanding in the curriculum and in inter school links; it is hardly surprising that it was bringing resistance in its wake.

Even when teachers were committed to implementing EMU, there were very real apprehensions about the experiential nature of the work. A group of teachers who had had four weeks away from school on an EMU course at Queen's University Belfast participated in a QPEP day workshop entitled 'Looking at Conflict'. Being aware of the workshop format, and the experiential nature of the day, when asked what their hopes and expectations were, the recurring theme of the responses was 'that they would survive it'.[16] During a subsequent exercise, participants' fears were elicited anonymously. Apprehensions about the ability of the individual concerned (or the rest of the group) to be honest, and the effect that such honesty or lack of it might have, were key concerns of the group. It could be claimed that the form of communication inherent in a workshop does not come easy to teachers. Another teacher made the comment that she as a primary school teacher spent the majority of her day without talking to another adult. As with communication and affirmation, co-operation is a key element of the workshop not only for the pupils, but for the adults involved themselves.

McCartney describes the constraints placed on the teachers, as individuals, as members of a profession and as employees of an institution. Such constraints include, the role of the school 'in supporting negative attitudes, alienation, loss of self-esteem, dependence on others'.[17] McKernan lists other possible constraints such as pupils beliefs and interest, fear of parental disapproval, lack of expertise, lack of support within the school.[18]

Just as a brick wall can be a dead end, or an obstacle to be overcome, so can constraints. In a beleaguered profession such as teaching, with ever increasing demands on the teacher's time and energy, EMU work in general can add to, rather than relieve teacher's stress. In addition the growing emphasis in the Northern Ireland Curriculum on cognitive, examinable skills, rather than affective areas of learning militate against involvement in 'low status' EMU work.

Additionally, teachers, as a profession are demoralised by the heavy demands on their time, are questioning their competence to take on new skills, and are insufficiently valued by society. And yet they are expected to be at the forefront of educational change, at the chalkface as it were.

Given the pressures, isolation and constraints that teachers operate under, it comes as no surprise that there is resistance to change.

QPEP's experience of training individual teachers to lead workshops demonstrated the value of the process for their own personal development; and presented a way to respond to educational change, in a way which affirms and empowers them. This experience led to more emphasis on in-service training in the second phase.

NOTES

1. Smith, Alan and Dunn, Seamus (1990) Extending Inter School Links' An evaluation of contact between Protestant and Catholic pupils in Northern Ireland, University of Ulster, Centre for the Study of Conflict.
2. Ibid.
3. Ibid.
4. O'Neill, Jim (1993) Final Report, Quaker Peace Education Project Evaluation, Charities Evaluation Services, December 1993
5. Hartop, Brendan (1994) Interviewed by Seamus Farrell, June 1994, Derry.

6. Northern Ireland Coucil for Education Developement (NICED) (1988) Education for Mutual Understanding - A Guide, NICED, Stranmillis.
7. Lampen, John (1990) Annual Report 1989/1990, Ulster Quaker Peace Education Project.
8. Smith, Alan and Dunn, Seamus (1990). Ibid.
9. Weissglass, Julian (1990) "Teachers have feelings too", Journal of Staff Development.
10. Bowers, Sue et al (1984) "Ways and Means - An Approach to Problem Solving", Kingston Friends Workshop Group.
11. Ibid.
12. Smith, Alan and Dunn, Seamus (1990) Ibid.
13. Weissglass, Julian (1990) Ibid.
14. Ibid.
15. McGranaghan, Pearse (1991) 'A Critical Appraisal', A Paper presented to the QPEP team 12.5.91.
16. Queen's University (1991) Day workshop at Queen's University fo EMU teachers, 24th January 1991.
17. McCartney, Clem (1984) 'Human Rights Education', A Paper prepared for the Standing Conference on Human Rights.
18. McKernan, James (1978) 'The Teaching of Controversial Issues, Beliefs, Attitudes and Values', NUU D Phil.

PART TWO

CHAPTER 9: TRANSITION FROM THE FIRST PHASE TO THE SECOND PHASE

When the Ulster Quaker Peace Education project was set up, the sponsoring body - the Ulster Quaker Peace Committee -had stated that after three years it would be seeking the advice of the QPEP management committee as to whether it should be "laid down", or continued. It was a unanimous decision on the part of the management committee that the project should be extended. The funds for the first phase of the project had been raised almost exclusively from non governmental, predominantly Quaker, sources. A new funding source, the Physical, Social and Economic Project (PSEP) was providing funding from the European Community for reconciliation and community relations projects. According an application made to this source through the Department of Education (DENI).

The volume of work, underlined the need for continuity of staff during the second phase, and the two posts created under the Action for Community Employment (ACE) scheme were made full-time for three years, and the existing fieldworker's post was elevated to Director. The result of the application for EC funding was that two of the three posts (Director and Workshop Facilitator) were grant-aided from PSEP funding, and the Administrator was supported by funding from DENI itself. For the second phase, I was appointed director, Eileen Healy - Workshop Facilitator and Sharon Moran -Resources Administrator.

The application to the EC identified four areas where initiatives would be taken, based on the previous three year's work.

Firstly, work with children and young people:-

1.1 Work with new age-ranges would be explored, for example children in P1, P2 and P3.

Workshops with P1 children were carried out in Omagh Integrated Primary School. As described in Chapter 10, QPEP created a workshop programme for a P3 class in Spring 1993, at Oakgrove Integrated Primary School.

1.2 New methods for involving young people in leading.

The idea of involving 6th formers in leading workshops with primary school children was mooted. This became a reality, for pragmatic reasons, in order to enable two integrated schools to qualify as an Education for Mutual Understanding (EMU) cross-community project, (see Chapter 10). As a deliberate attempt to involve and encourage leadership in older children, a group of secondary school children were invited to help the P7 conferences in 1992 and 1993.

1.3. Introducing mediation as a means of resolving conflict in the playground.

QPEP managed to embark on a pilot peer mediation project in September 1993, that was to become one of its most successful projects in terms of public recognition, and direct application of skills by children. Its initial training programme was thoroughly evaluated. The whole programme is explored in Chapter16, and a full report is being published by the Centre for the Study of Conflict at the same time as this report.

1.4 Identifying communities where our work in twinned schools could have a significant positive effect.

The first phase of the project had paved the way with work in Donemana and Castlederg where communities with a history of sectarian tension were deliberately chosen and QPEP had a pro-active role. In 1992 it was to work with three schools to enhance their existing EMU project, with a series of conflict resolution workshops ,(see Chapter 10).

1.5 The QPEP team would continue to be available for conflict resolution and prejudice reduction workshops, but with an added emphasis on teacher involvement, before during and afterwards.

There had been a tendency for schools, and other agencies to rely on QPEP to come in and have a regular input once a year, with a class of children, or on a joint programme. During the first phase, QPEP had welcomed these invitations as opportunities to try out new approaches, and was able to refine its programme as a result. Phase two with its emphasis on teacher involvement allowed QPEP to begin to insist on teacher involvement in the planning and delivery of workshops.

Secondly in the area of support for teachers/teacher training and training generally; it was clearly stated that work which involved passing on skills would take priority.

2.1 QPEP team training - a commitment to a regular programme to learn, practise, experiment with and evaluate leadership skills.

There would be a debate within QPEP about how much this was achieved. Nevertheless two evaluation weekends during the second phase (see Chapter 12) led by outside facilitators, and a series of eight half or day workshops in 1992-1993 augmented the regular planning/training QPEP team meetings. The intense training programme for QPEP staff and volunteers in the peer mediation project also added to the team's skills (see Chapter 16).

2.2 Teacher training and support during the establishment of EMU as a cross curricular theme.

Various attempts were made to establish teachers' support or advisory groups during the second phase. One effort resulted from a workshop by Professor Julian Weissglass at the ENCORE summer school in 1992, (see Chapter 13). QPEP was more successful in developing an in-service training (INSET) programme, and an innovation was the joint delivery of such programmes with a QPEP staff member and a teacher. Phase two enabled QPEP to develop and refine its INSET delivery. It was hoped to develop closer links with the Western Education and Library Board's own INSET programme, however this was not achieved in any systematic way.

QPEP was more successful in developing links with pre-service training, through contact with Stranmillis College. A day joint workshop with Stranmillis and St Mary's was undertaken for first year history students, by QPEP in 1993 and 1994.

It had been hoped to run a University Extra-Mural Certificate Course in Peace Education, at the University of Ulster, but this never took off, largely due to lack of people responding to the opportunity to do short term courses of evening classes.

2.3 Making training available to other people involved in group work, including short term membership of the QPEP team.

From time to time during 1991-1994 introductory courses were provided to inform other agencies in Derry about QPEP's work, with a view to their directing volunteers to the project. This had the desired effect of recruiting volunteers on a number of occasions.

2.4 Continuing and expanding links with the Peace Studies courses.

During Autumn 1991 QPEP was to have a significant input into the BA in Peace and Conflict Studies, at Magee College. The annual placement of a 3rd year Peace and Conflict Studies student aided the research component of the project. From time to time BA and MA students became active members of the QPEP team.

2.5 Adult Education.

Links already established with prisons, Corrymeela, Co-Operation North and other agencies were continued.

The third area of work in the second phase would be supporting and linking with similar agencies:-

3.1 Hosting the first summer school of the European Network for Conflict Resolution (ENCORE) .

Having been instrumental in the formation of ENCORE; QPEP played a significant role in hosting this summer school (see Chapter 13)

3.2 Continuing links with National Associate of the National Coalition Building Institute (NCBI).

By the time the second phase began, I had become a National Associate of the National Coalition Building Institute (NCBI). NCBI work was to play a large part in the development of QPEP during 1991-4, (see Chapter 14).

The fourth and final area was research and reporting:-

4.1 The Annual Report.

This was to continue in its extensive form; and in 1993 and 1994 the Management Committee took a more active role in editing it.

4.2 Articles for Journals about the work of the Project.

From the outset in 1988, an extra six months had been planned as a writing up period at the end of the project. From January 1994 the process of winding down workshops began, and during the final six months articles were published in a number of journals (see Appendix 3).

4.3 External Evaluation.

In 1993 the Management Committee commissioned the Charities Evaluation Services to carry out an external evaluation of the project, (see Chapter 15). The evaluation report published in December 1993 was to provide the basis for the establishment of a new project to carry on the work of QPEP.

4.4 Teacher's packs on conflict resolution and prejudice reduction.

A booklet was published by the project in 1992, about conflict resolution skills in primary schools - "Wee People". It was written by Eileen Healy and brought together a number of activities and exercises that QPEP had developed, noticeably "Dummy Bump", and the "House on Fire" model for explaining the "Iceberg principle" to younger children. It was seen as a useful resource by teachers as a source of prompts and ideas.

However QPEP did not attempt to produce materials that were designed to be directly relevant to the school curriculum. In the original discussions that led to the establishment of QPEP, there was an emphasis on the project's role being to interact with teachers rather than produce curriculum materials. QPEP relied on teachers to adapt and use exercises they had experienced on workshops. This would be an area that deserved addressing by a future project.

The second phase, aspects of which are described in detail in the following chapters, marked a transition. Whereas from 1988 - 91, the work focussed on children, without a pre-requisite of teacher involvement, opportunities were sought to work directly with teachers. QPEP had built up sufficient experience, and expertise, that it was more confident in asking for a partnership with teachers.

CHAPTER 10: WORK WITH CHILDREN AND YOUNG PEOPLE

1. Exploring new age-ranges and other innovations
In February 1993, the QPEP team were invited to work with the class teacher and her class of 6/7 year olds, at Oakgrove PS. The class teacher was committed to promoting an atmosphere of openness and appreciation in the class, and

> modelled what she wanted in the children, appreciating children's good work, behaviour, acts of kindness and generosity towards each other. Whenever appropriate, children played co-operative games rather than competitive games. She found that some children had great difficulty in thinking of any quality or attribute about themselves that they liked and impossible to think well of others.[1]

Although within the curriculum there seemed little opportunity for affirming the children, the class teacher believed that "it was a very necessary piece of work to be done in order for them to become whole rounded young people".[2]

The QPEP team (four in total) were invited to come into the school and to devise a programme for building, nurturing and encouraging self-worth and self-esteem. It was hoped that the class would begin to gel as a group, as a result. A planning meeting was held weekly and an evaluation carried out after each session.

This was different from QPEP's usual work in three respects; it was with a younger age-range, and concentrated on a single aspect of conflict resolution - self esteem. It was a challenge to focus an eight week series on this one theme. It also involved working alongside a teacher in her own classroom, the pedagogical dynamics of which are explored in a later chapter.

The space constraints of working in a small classroom, and the need to re-arrange furniture was sometimes disconcerting to the pupils. Games and ice-breakers were a crucial part of each session as they helped release some of their new-found energy which was brought up by a sudden change in teaching methods. Team-changes early on in the series caused a lack of continuity.

> Some children were shy and retiring to begin with but with time and with a real choice about participating, they opened up. It was interesting to see how the more lively children reacted. Initially they saw it as a situation where they had permission to be hyperactive but as the weeks went on they settled into the different way of doing things and became more responsible in their attitude.[3]

A measure of the success of the workshops was the growth in confidence of children in affirming each other and themselves. Because of the age of the children, the series gave the QPEP an opportunity to explore and develop new exercises. The partnership between teacher and facilitators was one of the successes of the series.

Individual initiatives

Individual volunteers took a pro-active approach in developing themes. For example, during the Gulf War, a workshop was run by members of the QPEP team, in conjunction with a local teacher, on "Children and War:- looking at feelings".

An innovation that was due to the enterprise of volunteer facilitator Jan Caspers was during "Why Waste Waste?" week in 1992. This was an environmental project devised by him, involving a class of pupils form each of four primary schools in Derry. It was jointly facilitated by QPEP workshop facilitators and community artists from the local Orchard gallery. The aim of the series of workshops was to explore ways of recycling waste. The project was enhanced by the creativity and imagination of the children involved; it illustrated the "close link that has to be built between 'peace education' and every part of the curriculum"[4]

Jan Caspers was instrumental too in setting up a follow-up meeting to a residential workshop in Rostrevor. Responding to a need to address the issue of whether a peace education workshop, having created "a temporary safe and open environment"[5] just leaves participants back where they came from, afterwards. At the end of the two day workshop, the sixth form participants were invited to leave their names if they were interested in carrying on the work started on the residential.

Jan Caspers, assisted by the Community Relations Officer for Armagh District Council, set up a follow up meeting. As a result the young people themselves organised follow-up activities. It was a powerful concrete example of effective support that assisted the participants in building on their workshop experience.

Eileen Healy, who was appointed full-time workshop facilitator in 1991 co-facilitated a "Time for Me" course in conjunction with the Women's Centre and the Workers Education Association (WEA). The course created a network of women in the Waterside area of Derry, and using skills training developed by through her work with QPEP "demonstrated the importance of the work of QPEP in the wider community" [6]

2. New methods for involving young people in leading

"An aspect of previous P7 conferences that we wished to retain was the concept of the children's ownership of their conference." [7] This policy was enhanced in 1992 and 1993 when QPEP invited different groups of secondary school aged children to have an input into the P7 conference. In 1992 a group devised role-play scenarios, based on their experience of going up into secondary school from primary school. Understandably this was an area of concern for many of the P7 participants. In 1993 a drama group of secondary school students acted out a conflict situation that required mediation.

In September 1991, Oakgrove Integrated Primary School opened in Derry. QPEP made contact with the school and offered its services, and as a result had an input into staff training, and also an innovative programme involving Oakgrove, and Belmont House, a school for children with special needs. Since both schools were integrated, they did not qualify for a DENI cross-community contact scheme on their own. By involving sixth formers from local state and catholic schools, the programme qualified for a grant, as well as providing leadership opportunities for older pupils. However as Seamus Farrell noted, "it was a matter of regret that it was only towards the end of the series that we gave serious attention to ways of involving the students more." [8] The overall project itself was to illustrate ways in which children can lead each other, whether able-bodied or disabled.

3. Identifying communities where our work in twinned schools could have a significant impact

In 1989 QPEP had approached two primary schools in Donemana, a community that had had a history of sectarian conflict, and had undertaken a programme of joint activities culminating in a residential at Corrymeela. In 1990/1 the two secondary schools in Castlederg had been approached for similar reasons, and a brief programme undertaken. However the schools concerned did not develop the joint programme further themselves.

In Spring 1992, QPEP was approached to have an input into a joint programme with three local schools, that were in walking distance of each other. However despite their geographical proximity, in terms of community relations they were were divided from each other. Prior to QPEP's involvement the three schools had shared school outings together, but the teachers agreed that very little contact was achieved by these. Specifically they didn't even mix on the bus, with friends from the same school "solidly sticking together".[9] QPEP conducted a series of workshops with the three schools, the impact of which was noticed by the teachers on a subsequent joint educational trip to the local railway museum. The children were "collaborating happily and excitedly in decision making and task allocation." [10]

It was a successful project, and a particularly well researched one. The recommendations from it included the critical role that teachers could play in providing the necessary back ground information. For example the fact that one of the schools had only recently become mixed gender had a profound effect. The need for the teachers to be actively involved in the planning and delivery of the workshops was paramount. This would avoid the situation where it was "easier for teachers to be observers and for QPEP to take sole charge of a programme than for both to develop a programme involving a co-leadership relationship". [11]

Other recommendations in relation to planning and evaluation were markers for a thorough methodology that was effectively put into practice in the pilot peer mediation programme in 1993/4. These concerned the need to process and take account of feedback from team members and children in planning subsequent workshops; detailed planning, training and rehearsal time. Mention was made of the value of a drama based approach. In the second phase of the overall project the essential role of the research aspect of action-research was demonstrably coming to the fore.

P7 conference developments

Whilst QPEP still ran the annual P7 conference, with a different theme each year, in 1991/4 each conference had an end product. In May 1991, the production of a wall 'newspaper' for the participants, entitled "The New World", dated 1996, and carrying news reports of "A world without weapons" was the result of the conference of that name. The following year, the subject of "Bullying" led to material from the conference being published as part of a chapter in a book edited by Delwyn Tatum. [12]

The most profound, far reaching effect of a P7 conference was obtained in 1993 on the subject of "Mediation". It was the influence of the children from the Model school who attended the conference which led to that school taking up the invitation to become involved in the subsequent peer mediation project. A booklet produced for that P7 conference, "Conflict Busters" proved to be a useful resource subsequently. [13] More will be said about this in Chapter 16.

Finally in 1994, following in the tradition of giving eleven year olds the opportunity to be heard, the theme of the conference was "We want to be heard". It was filmed by Ulster Television, and broadcast as a news item. In the words of one of the 11 year old participants the final session of the day was when "all of the groups came into a big room. Everything we learnt we had to do it all out in front of everybody". [14] A panel of four adults listened to the concerns of the children; the panel were impressed and moved by the compassion, concern and creative ways the children communicated.

NOTES

1. Healy, Eileen and Maher, Berenice (1994) "Nurturing Self Esteem" Unpublished article
2. Ibid.

3. Ibid.
4. Caspers, Jan (1992) p14 Annual Report 1991/2, QPEP, Derry.
5. Caspers, Jan (1992) p22 Annual Report 1991/2, QPEP, Derry.
6. Healy, Eileen (1992) p47 Annual Report 1991/2, QPEP, Derry.
7. Lindsay, John (1992) p 20 Annual Report 1991/2, QPEP, Derry.
8. Farrell, Seamus (1992) p 11 Annual Report 1991/2, QPEP, Derry.
9. Farrell, Seamus (1992) p 12 Annual Report 1991/2, QPEP, Derry.
10. Farrell, Seamus (1992) p 13 Annual Report 1991/2, QPEP, Derry.
11. IBID.
12. Lampen, John and Farrell, Seamus (1993) The Ulster Quak Peace Education Project in Countering Bullying, Ed Tattum and Herbert, Trentham Press.
13. Lampen, John, (1993) Conflict Busters, QPEP
14. Porter, Russell (aged 11) (1995) p30 Annual Report 1993/4, QPEP

CHAPTER 11: INVOLVING TEACHERS MORE CLOSELY IN THE WORK

Although we can challenge teachers with new curriculum, different visions, suggestions for change and research results, we must do more. We must provide them with the opportunity to reflect on their assumptions and beliefs about education, construct their own understanding of proposed changes, work through their feelings that inhibit their ability to change and make their own decisions about how to respond. [1]

During the first phase QPEP had acknowledged the need to close the gap between an informal team of adults coming in to do a workshop, and the everyday relationship between the teacher and his/her class.

our work needs to be more closely integrated into the on-going work of the classroom....we cannot expect teachers to reproduce the impact of six or seven people coming into the school for a day and doing unconventional things with the class.[2]

QPEP was committed to supporting teachers. During the second phase QPEP explored various ways of giving support including the provision of adequate follow-up materials as part of a post workshop package and an opportunity for teachers to express their feelings about the many changes that seemed to be forced upon them.

In-Service Training

"Why", said the Dodo to Alice, "the best way to explain it is to do it."
(Lewis Carroll).

In 1991, QPEP ran two linked training days -"Myself and Others; making Education for Mutual Understanding meaningful". These provided an opportunity for teachers to explore and experience the methodology behind the exercises in a typical workshop. The days also led to workshops being conducted at participant's schools. One teacher commented on the QPEP team, writing "they are committed to their work, and ....have great respect and understanding for those who are trying to embark on EMU".[3]

Since 1990 QPEP had a regular input into Queen's University Belfast's In-Service course for teachers on the educational themes of EMU and Cultural Heritage. In the 1993/4 Annual Report, the course tutor, Norman Richardson wrote about this input,

> the teachers' responses were positive, and many expressed appreciation of being able to deal with "Understanding Conflict" (one of the basic objectives of EMU) in an active and practical manner. The particular activities covered in the brief sessions focussed on listening, affirmation and co-operation. Some of the teachers indicated that they would use the activities in their own work. There was also some evidence, in the teachers' subsequent coursework submissions, of actual incorporation of certain of these activities into programmes of work.[4]

It was clear then, that QPEP could present its experience to teachers in such a way that they could subsequently take ideas and use them in the class room. In this regard the QPEP publication "Wee People - conflict resolution exercises for primary schools"[5] was widely appreciated. However in the overall evaluation of the project, O'Neill makes the point that "one of the main issues that emerged from the findings was the lack of relevance of QPEP's methods to specific parts of the school curriculum".[6]

This begs the question of whether the methods were irrelevant, or whether QPEP had been ineffective in making the link with the curriculum. Smith, in a report on a conference entitled "The EMU promoting school", argued that it was precisely the skills of an interactive approach that was necessary for teachers to be effective,

> many teachers would welcome training and support which would strengthen their confidence in the emotive and affective aspects to learning which come to the fore through themes such as EMU[7]

QPEP had a wealth of experience in this area; and there were obvious links between its work programme of conflict resolution skills training and the aims of EMU,

> learn(ing) to respect and value themselves and others; appreciat(ing) the interdependence of people within society; appreciat(ing) the benefits of resolving conflict by nonviolent means.[8]

Equally importantly the consultation paper for EMU as a cross-curricular theme specified that teaching and learning styles "associated with (EMU) are experiential and interactive rather than received and passive." NICC Likewise it stresses the need to encourage skills such as "listening, co-operating, contributing", and describes the role of the teacher

> as facilitator (encouraging) a climate of caring and mutual respect - a sense of achievement for each pupil - a co-operative as much as a competitive atmosphere - increased group and individual responsibility - understanding using and transferring learning skills.[9]

Clearly QPEP's expertise is demonstrably relevant to the above teaching style, however the CES evaluation was to indicate that QPEP's relevance to curricular subjects was not so obvious.

Teachers have become experts in relating subjects, topics etc to the curriculum, and any future project would do well to harness this expertise. It was noticeable that as teachers became more enthusiastic about the workshop approach, particularly in the context of mediation, they started to make intuitive links with the curriculum. Talking and listening skills, immediately sprang to mind, in the context of English.

QPEP was able to inspire that level of enthusiasm in a workshop, by developing an approach with teachers that reduced stress.

In their visits to the former Soviet Union, John Lampen and other QPEP volunteers, had explored ways of involving groups of teachers as observers in the workshops whilst still maintaining the integrity of the experience for the pupils.

Gradually a three stage format evolved for QPEP's in-service programmes with teachers. It was used successfully with staffs of individual schools, with consortia training with the North Eastern Education and Library Boards and on pre-service EMU courses with students from Stranmillis and St Mary's Colleges.

The first stage of the workshop would comprise a mini-workshop where the ground rules would be established, exercises of affirmation, co-operation and communication undertaken, and the methodology of the "iceberg principle" explained.

The next stage provided an opportunity for each participant to reflect on a series of questions, each one with a different partner.

> The teachers are invited to consider from their own school experience how they were mistreated and how they were helped, then going on to acknowledge their own strengths as teachers and the support they might need from colleagues. This evoked powerful memories and consequent reflection on our current ways of being in schools[10]

This exercise called "concentric circles", generated a high level of listening, and sharing, and was enjoyed by teachers.

The concluding part of the process was "peer training" whereby the participants were split into groups and each group given an activity to lead the others in. They had a short time to prepare how to introduce it. The rest of the group was encouraged to take an active part.

The rationale for the three stages was based on a theory of educational change developed by Julian Weissglass.[11] He posited the idea that there were four inter dependent elements in educational change, and they could be visualised as the apexes of a tetrahedron or pyramid. Firstly there was a need to get new information (this is represented by the mini workshop phase of the programme). There is also a requirement to take action - opportunity for this is given in the final "peer training" element of the agenda. Time for reflection and planning is a third key aspect, represented by the preparation for leading. The final significant ingredient in educational change is emotional support. Emotional support essentially is listening, and in this context, on a one-to -one basis which allows for the expression of feelings. The concentric circles activity creates an environment of emotional support.

However the term "support" was not generally understood by teachers - as Lampen noted, when the participants were asked what type of support they needed, the participants "immediately reverted to the relation of the administration to the school.....the need for personal support that had emerged during the concentric circles exercises, tended to get lost," [12]

In 1992 QPEP capitalised on the impact of the ENCORE summer school by agreeing to a request to assist St Columb's College in Derry in the provision of a conflict resolution package as part of their Pastoral Care programme. The head of sixth form having made the initial approach began "to worry what I was letting myself and my colleagues in for." [13] when he saw the programme. In the QPEP annual report he wrote that

> (at the end of the trial workshop with 6th form tutors) my only concern was that I had displayed so little trust in (QPEP). It had been the most enjoyable and worthwhile Baker Day that the participants had been involved in. [14]

Subsequently the entire school staff of over 100, divided into four groups did a half day workshop each as part of the planning and delivery of the conflict resolution unit. From informal feedback on the day, it was clear that the teachers acknowledged the universal appeal of the particular workshop approach and content. Nevertheless the delivery of INSET for a unit for a whole school approach to conflict resolution is a long term goal, and QPEP needs to have a distinct plan as to how to best support such a programme. Otherwise either resources and staff time can be tied up in a major project at a single school, or else QPEP is unable to deliver enough support to make it s involvement in a programme viable.

Supporting teachers

During the second phase the QPEP team put a lot of thought into how to allow teachers to express their feelings about the stress they were undoubtedly under, through having to come to terms with the changes in the N Ireland curriculum. It was vital that any exercises were demonstrably relevant, and non threatening. Often the QPEP team had to deal with initial resistance from unwilling participants. On one particular occasion one principal who passed on the first exercise of the day - an affirmation activity - saying that "I was brought up to believe that self praise was no praise at all" [15], enthusiastically joined in a co-operation exercise at the end.

The three stage workshop generally transformed teachers from being participant observers to being leaders, and in the process reduced stress.

Support groups

In Autumn 1992, motivated by the success of Julian Weissglass' workshop at the European Network for Conflict Resolution in Education (ENCORE)ENCORE Summer School, an attempt was made to set up a support group for educational change. Unfortunately this petered out. more imaginative ways are necessary to involve teachers in support groups.

Working with individual teachers

In the previous chapter there was an example of how the QPEP team worked with a p3 class, on the theme of self-esteem, alongside the teacher in her own classroom.It ilustrated how a working relationship between the QPEP team and a class teacher could evolve, in support of the teacher.

Although, by her own admission, the class teacher was expecting miracles from the QPEP team,

> as the weeks progressed it became clear the QPEP team were a back-up to what I was already doing in the classroom and not the reverse. It was that they slotted into what I was trying to achieve rather than me fitting into what they needed. The major advantage of having the team in was the increased ratio of adults to children which made individual and small group work much more effective[16]

Nevertheless having extra adults in the teacher's own classroom posed its own problems, As the class teacher, I was unsure whether to leave discipline to the team or to interject and maintain order." However, on reflection she decided that, "the team was made up mostly of volunteers who had no specific training in classroom teaching and communication with young children." Consequently she decided to not to be a passive observer. As a result the workshops improved, as she "knew the children best and was able to draw them out in discussion."

This teacher also deliberated about the way the team and she complemented each other.

> What I brought to the team was my experience of working with small children. Advantages for me in participation were many, I got the chance to spend more time with a small group and listen to what they had to say in a way that I would never have done on a ratio of 1:28. I observed children who were normally quite shy and quiet opening up and gaining confidence. The children had more opportunities for talking about their feelings[17]

Caspers writing about the same series of workshops argues that in general if the workshop ignores the

> negative aspects of (the school and home environment)...the workshop is put in a kind of splendid isolation that renders most of its achievements useless in a host environment that bears little resemblance to the world, or the world view of the workshop[18]

This need to ensure that the workshop experience is seen as an integral part of the school, and yet not constrained by it, has been met on occasions by school staff INSET days being co-led by a teacher and a QPEP team member.

Responding to invitations to come and work in a school

With its new resolve to actively involve teachers in every aspect of the programme, as a pre-requisite to its taking on a workshop in the school, QPEP was faced with a recurring problem. This was timetabling meetings with teachers. Invariably spells of 40 minutes or so were the maximum periods available, at the end of the day. In any group of staff there would be levels of enthusiasm ranging from highly motivated to mandated.

In Spring 1992, as a result of its input in a workshop for pastoral care teachers in Coleraine, QPEP had an invitation to work with a the whole year group of 6th formers for the purpose of "promoting co-operation and understanding among (them), in preparation for their final year at school"[19]

An experiential planning meeting with the staff gave them a taste of the subsequent workshop with the young people. The latter was successful, and included opportunities for continuous feedback from the participants, through the use of "graffiti charts" and evaluations. A three week gap between workshops allowed for the processing of evaluations and feedback, and a meeting with the teachers.

This meeting allowed for the teachers' fears to be addressed - and often teachers had fears particularly about the level of sharing required from participants, and how this might make them vulnerable. This fear was specified in Farrell's research.

> At the planning meeting with the teachers we addressed the fears around our proposals for the second workshop. These envisaged students sharing with each other much more deeply about themselves than usual. The fear was expressed that students who did take this risk..would have it used against them by others subsequently and that a dread about this happening would create a mood of resistance to the whole process.[20]

However Farrell went on to point out that "underlying our concern about the risk for students was our own fear of taking risks". A key role for QPEP to play was to listen to such fears, and demonstrate that they had been taken into consideration in planning the programme, and to only take calculated risks The success of this approach was illustrated by the evaluations of the young people, following a powerful use of the Dummy Bump exercise, adapted for the first time for teenagers, comments were evoked like, "'I didn't realise the consequences of slagging'. 'Some people are totally lonely because of it'. 'Instead of slagging people make them feel wanted'."[21]

These workshops were seminal in incorporating the research data, generated before, during and after the first workshop in the delivery of the second; it was an example of how QPEP could have an effective role as action-research project, and that it took into consideration Jan Caspers' concern about workshops being in splendid isolation of the school environment. By focussing on specific areas during the limited time of the staff meetings, it made the best use of them, and ensured that the teachers were heard, and therefore better able to "own" the whole process.

Whole school approach

QPEP's links with Oakgrove Integrated Primary School, which opened in September 1991, provided a context to experiment with whole school approaches. As its principal, Anne Murray was to write,

> In a very practical way (QPEP) have given us tools to put our aims of integration and child-centredness into action. Our whole school esteem is healthier because of their generous input.[22]

In the first year of Oakgrove's existence, QPEP had worked with each of the classes, put on a workshop for parents and conducted an INSET day for staff. The following school year they had supported an individual teacher with her p3 class, and in 1993/4 had introduced a peer mediation project into the school. The latter required the active support and participation of the lunchtime supervisors.

Pre-service training

St Mary's College and Stranmillis College are "unequivocally committed to the promotion of Education for Mutual Understanding among young people in the schools and colleges of the province."[23]

As was often to be the case, an input into a conference or workshop led to QPEP being invited to lead a workshop or series of workshops with other bodies. As the result of her attendance at an "EMU in Transition" conference in Newcastle, Shirley Magowan, a lecturer at Stranmillis College, invited QPEP to undertake a day's workshop at with first year history students, from Stranmillis and St Mary's.

The day was evaluated and although it was rated as "effective" in mixing the two groups of students, it was only seen as "average" in terms of relevance to EMU, and building confidence to lead exercises in the classroom. It is clear that the day began to open up possibilities, and with the increased emphasis on teacher involvement on future projects arising from QPEP, a coordinated attempt to develop such training is required.

By the end of its second phase, QPEP had developed a workshop format that enabled teachers to express their feelings of disquiet and apprehension at the start, experience the fun and stimulation of a workshop, and begin to visualise ways they could put the exercises into practice themselves, in the classroom. This was a considerable achievement, given the resistance to such an approach, by teachers who were often mandated to attend. The format needs to be demonstrably related to the curriculum.

NOTES

1. Weissglass, Julian (1991) "Teachers have feelings too", Journal of Staff Development, (1991.)
2. Lampen, John p 45 (1991) Annual Report 1990/1, QPEP, Derry.
3. Hamilton, Cynthia, p 10 (1991) Annual Report 1990/1, QPEP, Derry.
4. Richardson, Norman, p 32 (1994) Annual Report 1993/4, QPEP
5. Healy, Eileen (1992) Wee People, QPEP, Derry
6. O'Neill, Jim, p55 (1993) Quaker Peace Education Project Evalution, Final Report, Charities Evaluation Services, Belfast.
7. Smith, Alan, (1994) The EMU Promoting School, conference report, Centre for the Study of Conflict, University of Ulster, Coleraine.
8. Northern Ireland Coucil for Education Developement (NICED) (1988) Education for Mutual Understanding - A Guide, NICED, Stranmillis.
9. Northern Ireland Curriculum Council (NICC) Analysis of the Educ tional Theme of Education for Mutual Understanding NICC , 1992
10. Hegan, Judith p51 (1993) Annual Report 1992/3, QPEP, Derry.
11. Weissglass, Julian (1991) Ibid.
12. Lampen, John p 54 (1993) Annual Report 1992/3, QPEP, Derry.
13. Rainey , Gerry, p55 (1993) Annual Report 1992/3, QPEP, Derry.
14. Ibid.
15. Tyrrell, Jerry (1994) "Affirmation, co-operation......." Journal of Community Relations Council, Spring 1994.
16. Healy, Eileen and Maher, Berenice (1994) "Nurturing Self Esteem" Unpublished article.
17. Ibid.
18. Caspers, Jan, p 13 (1993) Annual Report 1992/3, QPEP, Derry.
19. Hegan, Judith p24 (1993) Annual Report 1992/3, QPEP, Derry.
20. Farrell, Seamus, p 26 (1992) Annual Report 1991/2, QPEP, Derry.
21. Ibid.
22. Murray, Anne p 16 (1992) Annual Report 1991/2, QPEP, Derry.
23. Magowan, Shirley p 61 (1993) Annual Report 1992/3, QPEP

CHAPTER 12: TRAINING AND ROLE OF THE QPEP TEAM

Within a month of its existence, QPEP had started to provide internal training for its own volunteers. During the initial stages of the project this was to be a vital ingredient in its success - there was a need for volunteers and staff to gain in confidence and competence in order to deliver the workshop programme. This process is described in the Chapter 3. As collective experience built up there was no longer such an urgent need to be trained to facilitate new programmes. A recurring complaint by team members, was that the team was relying too much on only one or two models, and not being adventurous in experimenting with new approaches.

To a degree this was true, but with an average of 3 workshops a week, there was a natural tendency to rely on old familiar exercises. The workshop schedule sometimes militated against innovation. Conversely the demands of a particular agencies required QPEP to adapt and custom build an approach to meet an agency's needs. This was particularly true of QPEP's input into Co-Operation North's "Ourselves and Others" programme, and individual conferences requiring effective interaction by participants, (EMU in Transition, US Holidays, and Centre for the Study of Conflict).

Nevertheless it was often the perception of the QPEP volunteer team that there were not adequate opportunities for exposure to new approaches. Accordingly in 1992/3 the staff workshop facilitator organised a series of day and half day training workshops for the QPEP team run by outside facilitators. A list of them illustrates the variety and breadth - Drama; Understanding Conflict and Ways Out of It; Group Work Skills; Prejudice Awareness; Bubble Dialogue - (a computer programme); Mediation; Conflict Partnership Process.

The final project of QPEP, the pilot peer mediation project, was a logical development from the conflict resolution skills training that QPEP had been involved in from the outset. However for most of the team it was a new departure. It therefore necessitated the QPEP team being trained in the very processes that they were expected to train the children themselves, almost simultaneously.[1]

Evaluation/Professional Development weekend

In addition to the various internal, and external training opportunities created for the QPEP team, there were two residential evaluation weekends during the second phase of the project.

The first one, in November 1991 at Benburb conference centre, was facilitated by Dave Duggan. It involved a mixture of exercises using art to explore concepts of leadership, and opportunities to discuss an agenda drawn up in response to a questionnaire completed by the participants and returned prior to the weekend. A report of the weekend included detailed recommendations that illustrate the commitment of the individual members of the QPEP team to the development and improvement of the project.[2]

The need for QPEP to have agreed conflict resolution processes for its own conflicts was signalled. Other recommendations concerned the need for clarification about action research, and a commitment to try and reach more adults. A consensus was beginning to emerge about the need to "Irishize" the NCBI model, and for QPEP to disengage from NCBI and develop its own model. The role of QPEP in the development of NCBI in Northern Ireland is explored in Chapter 14.

The image of the Quaker Peace Education Project, the logo, and the name - these were key issues for the participants. Those who identified as Quakers were in a small minority in the QPEP team. Although historically Quakers had played a significant role in the peace movement, the bulk of volunteers and staff did not come from that tradition. Nevertheless the sponsor of the project was the Ulster Quaker Peace Committee. The external evaluation of the project came to the conclusion that generally "there were mixed responses to the name Quaker in the project title ....on the whole the term Quaker was seen as being neutral within the Northern Ireland context and appeared to be more an asset than a hindrance."[3]

QPEP's involvement of volunteers had been pragmatic, and unique amongst action research projects at the Centre for the Study of Conflict at the University. There was a growing awareness that attention needed to be given to defining the role and structures for payment of volunteer facilitators. Throughout the project there was a tension between the volunteers who saw themselves as being the people who were active at the "chalk face" and who were involved on a day to day basis, and the management committee who fulfilled a different function, of ensuring that the project kept on course, and that the staff were accountable, etc. There was an attempt to clarify the decision making process. Part of this tension was caused by the difference between what QPEP was set up to be - an action research project with one member of staff as part of the Centre for the Study of Conflict and therefore part of the hierarchy of the University of Ulster - and what it appeared to be to volunteers. The latter perception was one of a dynamic, consensus seeking, democratic organisation.

During workshops this was achievable. Outside workshops the difference in status between staff and volunteers was a symptom of the inegalitarian reality. As volunteers became more and more committed to the work, they became more and more aware of the contradiction.

Added to this was the perception that the QPEP team were facilitating conflict resolution skills training workshops, but were not necessarily practising what they preached. The fact that there was not a consensus within the QPEP team about the role of affirmation in tackling conflict for example, illustrated the divisions within it.

Although some QPEP team volunteers would feel that the project was dependant on them, the wellbeing of the QPEP team was secondary to the real clients of the project, the different agencies and schools that provided the participants of the workshops. Any future project carrying on the work deserves to make clear its expectations of volunteers; and to have clear lines of communication and decision making, particularly in relation to grievances.

The final QPEP team evaluation weekend, in Downings, Co Donegal in February 1993, facilitated by Marie Quiery attempted to deal with conflicts within the QPEP team. The weekend had been prepared for by a day workshop of group work skills training, and by a questionnaire. These had led to a threefold aim for the weekend:-

1. To evaluate the past year's work of the Project and set goals for the coming year.

2. To discuss the common issues and problems for the staff and volunteers.

3. To explore the practice base for the Project, and suggest improvements for its operation.[4]

Having listed achievements, an often painful process of listing and discussing frustrations began, with the staff and volunteers being able to draw up an action plan by the end of the weekend. The general goals for the remaining months of the project were

Consolidate the theory and practice of models; thrash out ideologies; gear workshops to research and teachers' needs; voice new ideas; look at gaps in the ages we work with and models used; set up support groups for development; discuss involvement of under-represented (client) groups; improve communication within the organisation; find a speedy and effective way of dealing with conflict - learn to let go.[5]

There were specific recommendations;

to have a standard application form for volunteers; to set up a pilot mediation project in schools; support for volunteer facilitators, eg payment; record our work, eg Annual Report.[6]

In the event some of these recommendations were put into practice, notably the application form, and ending QPEP with a major project - the peer mediation project, and gearing workshops to teacher and research needs. A member of the Management Committee (John Lampen) was present as a member of the QPEP team of staff and volunteers. Nevertheless the evaluation weekend could only make recommendations, it had no decision making role within the organisation.

During the first phase of the project the informal relationship between the University and the management committee in the running of the project, and between the staff and volunteers generally worked well.

During the second phase it began to show signs of strain. The management committee had no status within the University; yet it employed two staff and took the decisions in relation to the running of the project. The director was employed by the University, it was not clear who the volunteers were responsible to, nor was there a clear grievance procedure for volunteers.

This led to a situation that when a conflict arose between staff and volunteers, formal procedures had to be put into place afterwards; this was commented on by Jim O'Neill in his evaluation. Lampen was to maintain that if O'Neill's recommendations "had been in place from the beginning, we would simply have had a lot mote bureaucracy but not better management - because of the nature of the creature we were managing"[7]

Ultimately what marked the Ulster Quaker Peace Education Project from other research projects within the University was its links with the local community. It actively encouraged volunteers, some of whom had no academic qualifications, and it developed something of the ethos of a voluntary organisation, but within the constraints of a limited project lifespan, and limited opportunities for effecting change.

The QPEP team members had a profound effect on the project itself; they were the individuals who put the theory in to practice, who fed back their hopes and their complaints and improvements. They were fiercely committed to the work, and strived to ensure that a high quality was maintained. Any future project arising out of QPEP needs to ensure that the role of volunteers within the project was clearly defined, and the clarify the agency's expectations of its volunteers.

NOTES

1. Farrell, Seamus & Tyrrell, Jerry(1995) Report o n a Peer Mediation Pilot Project - Centre for the Study of Conflict , University of Ulster
2. Schlindwein, Helena , (1991) Action Research of QPEP Professional Development Weekend, 1/3 November 1991 (Unpublished)
3. O'Neill, Jim (1993)
4. Quiery , Marie, (1993) Report on Evaluation Weekend at Downings, Co Donegal
5. Ibid.
6. Ibid.
7. Lampen, John (1994) Transcript of an interview. 3.3.94.

CHAPTER 13: THE EUROPEAN NETWORK FOR CONFLICT RESOLUTION IN EDUCATION (ENCORE) SUMMER SCHOOL.

From 18th -22nd July 1992 the Ulster Quaker Peace Education Project undertook one of its most ambitious projects, the hosting of the first Summer School of the European Network for Conflict Resolution in Education (ENCORE). The venue was Magee College at the University of Ulster.

The idea of the summer school had been first mooted at the initial meeting of ENCORE in September 1990. By the following Autumn QPEP had prepared a draft programme , and agreement was sought from ENCORE members at their September 1991 meeting in Brussels. The title of the summer school was "Values in Conflict - Education for Change". The format of the summer school brought together complementary pedagogical approaches. There were three keynote speakers, who gave their talks in a lecture theatre, and twelve separate workshops lasting 3 hours, using an experiential approach. Financial support from Derry City Council's "Initiative 92" programme underwrote the cost of the conference, and a grant from the Department of Education paid for a conference dinner. A donation from the Joseph Rowntree Charitable Trust substantially helped towards the participation of individuals from the former Eastern Europe.

The bulk of the data for the first section of this chapter is from individual evaluations by participants.

Publicity

Advance notice of the conference was being circulated in English and German by Autumn 1991. In March 1992 a three colour leaflet in English, German and French, was launched at a reception at Magee College by Professor Robert Gavin, Provost of Magee, Councillor Noel McKenna representing the Mayor of Derry and Jerry Tyrrell, Summer School Director.

The leaflet gave a synopsis of ten workshops and details of the three keynote speakers, and the chairperson of the conference. There was some concern expressed in evaluations of the summer school that the delay in disseminating this information had led to fewer participants taking part. Nevertheless there were over 60 participants from 12 different countries, including 10 from former Eastern European countries.

The logistics of organising the final programme meant that it wasn't distributed until a week before the event - in some cases it arrived after people had left. There was some confusion with booking arrangements.

Participation

Although Britain and Ireland were well represented and others came from Belgium and Germany it was noticeable that France, the Netherlands (with a strong history of conflict resolution skills), Italy and Scandinavia were not represented. This was symptomatic of ENCORE'S strengths and weaknesses in terms of networking. The number of Northern Irish participants was appreciated - and was felt to help ground the event. Several people felt it had a good balance of global/local people.

Date and length

The workshop began lasted five days. Although it was timed well for N Irish teachers, who were on holiday, it was still term time for teachers in England. Generally it was felt that the length was adequate. There were suggestions that in the future after a summer school it would have been a good idea to visit schools where practical work could be tried out or seen.

Programme Content

One presenter expressed a consensus view about the programme as "Good balance between the head, the heart and the spirit. Space to think, to feel, to be with excellent intellectual inputs and space to dance and reflect."

However frustration was expressed by participants about only being able to attend three out of twelve workshops. Some indicated that workshops should be repeated, particularly where a change in the original programme meant that it was impossible to attend one's original choice of workshop. However the point was made that " the strongest impression was of the very similar way in which peace education is developing in so many places" Tyrrell For this reason feedback recommended that workshop leaders should discuss methods with each other beforehand, to avoid repetition.

Well planned workshops that related to real issues happening now, eg

reunification in Germany; sectarianism in N Ireland were appreciated.
One participant wrote that

> None of the three workshops I chose focussed on education in the
> institutional sense at all. It would have helped me a little more if
> all workshops related to education structures and not just to
> conflict resolution/mediation generally, I did enjoy and profit
> from all though.

This point was reinforced by the comment "Need to discuss *the how* and
not just *the what* ie How can this happen in schools? What are the
approaches to use?"

There was difficulty about pitching the content at the right level; in an
evaluation by members of ENCORE immediately after the summer
school the question was raised "Who was (the summer school) for, and
what was its purpose?"[1]

Another comment identified a key issue, "Many of us are interested in
each other's work but are now more advanced and may want something
more specialised in our field."

In essence there was a need for "beginning" and "advanced" workshops
because there was a need to work from where people are at, ie different
levels. . There was recognition that a basic level was fine 'for spreading
the word and bringing more people in" and thus teaching new skills.
ENCORE gatherings could also be a useful forums for trying out new
ideas and new methods with ENCORE members in a knowledgeable but
critical atmosphere. Nevertheless the programme was found to be too
rudimentary for people who have a lot of experience in this area already;
and a desire for more time for "talking about our work and our problems
(rather) than doing the same exercises we do anyway at home"..

One highlight for all concerned was the Market Place. This was an area
where people could display posters, resources, show videos and talk to
people about their work. It was also accessible to day visitors to the
summer school.

Keynote Speeches

As previously mentioned there was an attempt to mix experiential workshops with more didactic, formal presentations. There was a lot of positive feedback about the key note speakers. "Very well prepared key note addresses with warm, committed people giving them". A suggestion was made that a follow-up workshop be directly related to a each lecture. (Julian Weissglass had already agreed to do so)

Accommodation

This was the only aspect of the summer school that proved to be a negative experience for some participants. The conference dinner however, was a delight for many.

Location

"Placed in a context which was a constant reminder of work to be done" summed up the view that the venue and N I dimension and immediate contact with Derry were much appreciated.

Leisure Programme

The evaluations stressed the need for a gathering place for social events. Although effort had been put into a social programme for the Sunday night and the final night, other evening entertainment was left up to the participants themselves. There was a strong recommendation that the first night should have been structured to allow for informal introductions. This would have made a big difference to the atmosphere and to starting relationships. ' "Going off to the pub" seemed to be one of the few options, and it was clear that people felt excluded if they "weren't in the know", or if for cultural or other reasons it was not appropriate for them to drink alcohol'.

The net result of a lack of an organised social programme led to one person writing that

> I felt I never had a chance to see and hear other participants together until the end. Had we had a better sense of identity and a gathering place the free time could have been improved.

The Ceilidh on the final night was universally appreciated. There were opportunities for individuals to go on a walking tour of the city, and to visit the local Peace and Reconciliation Group. The feedback about this was that "Irish touches (were) not only educational from a cultural point of view but helped to bring the participants together".

Administration/Organisation

The team of QPEP staff and volunteers were praised for their helpfulness, co-operation and friendliness and general hospitality. This plus the reciprocal attitude of the participants led to the following comment. "I thought that the school was very successful and there was a nice warm atmosphere- which is not usual at such events".

ENCORE as an organisation wrote "For a first attempt...ENCORE felt that the Summer School was a great success".[2]

NOTES

All quotations form ENCORE Summer School, Evaluations (1992), Ulster Quaker Peace Education Project, Derry.except
1. Bentley, Marigold (1992) Notes of ENCORE network, 22/7/92, Derry
2. Ibid.

CHAPTER 14: THE ROLE OF QPEP IN THE DEVELOPMENT OF THE WORK OF THE NATIONAL COALITION BUILDING INSTITUTE (NCBI) IN NORTHERN IRELAND

In 1988, Cherie Brown founder and director of the National Coalition Building Institute International (NCBI) in the USA was invited to Northern Ireland to lead the first of what were to be six annual Training the Trainer weekends in Prejudice Reduction. As QPEP field worker I became involved in NCBI work from the first of these weekends. The NCBI prejudice reduction model, and its model for tackling controversial issues, subsequently formed a significant part of QPEP's work, with secondary school students and adults.

This chapter will explore how the relationship between QPEP and NCBI developed, and what was learnt from the practice of using NCBI processes in Northern Ireland.

The 1988 weekend had been organised by the forerunner of The Mediation Network for Northern Ireland (MNNI). The following year QPEP took an active role in organising the weekend, out of which a network of leaders was born, known as "OCTOPUS",

In 1990 QPEP organised the NCBI training weekend jointly with Youth Action Northern Ireland. A report of the event in the form of a booklet "Prejudice Reduction - a workshop approach"[1] by Will Pegg, staff member of QPEP, became a popular resource for trainers in N Ireland.

In 1991 QPEP undertook the organisation of the weekend on behalf of "OCTOPUS". By 1992, "OCTOPUS" was taking on more of a leading role, and the following year opened a separate bank account as NCBI N Ireland, though the administration of the now annual workshop led by Cherie Brown was done through the QPEP office.

In 1990 I became National Associate in N Ireland for NCBI, and as such was responsible for developing OCTOPUS as a chapter of NCBI. During the period 1990-94,this involved spending four days each year at a meeting of all the National Associates in Boston, and later Washington DC, and assisting in the leading of prejudice reduction and leadership training workshops there. Because of the seminal role that NCBI workshops had within the QPEP programme, being National Associate was part of my QPEP work.

The bulk of the work of OCTOPUS was done by the QPEP team. The consistent support from Cherie Brown and NCBI International for local NCBI leadership in N Ireland was exemplified by her annual visits which became a focus for developmental work. These together with visits by myself and other NCBI chapter members to NCBI National Associates meetings in the USA established a strong transatlantic link.

The link between QPEP and NCBI processes differed from that with other conflict resolution processes because as well as playing a key role in establishing NCBI in N Ireland, most of the QPEP staff and volunteers became an integral part of NCBI N Ireland itself. The NCBI prejudice reduction process emphasises welcoming diversity, encouraging participants to take pride in their heritage, and assisting the development of empathy between opposing groups with the ultimate goal of building alliances. In most of its programmes with young people of 13+, and adults QPEP, endeavoured to use NCBI processes. During the six years of the project, over 100 groups, 6th formers, peace and reconciliation agencies, teachers, youth workers, participated in NCBI workshops led by the QPEP team. This provided a wealth of experience that NCBI processes had a profound effect on people's attitude to prejudice.

It is appropriate here to try and identify how NCBI processes differed from other conflict resolution approaches. The goal of NCBI processes was to build alliances between traditionally opposed groups; a key element in this process, although not reached nor necessarily sought after in every workshop was that of "emotional healing". There was recognition that a personal experience of injustice often became the basis for a prejudice towards another group; through sharing personal stories a greater understanding and empathy was engendered between groups. As McKittrick has already pointed out

> This work raised my self-awareness about the role of emotion in group activity. I began to see how important it was to create the right conditions if difficult personal experiences were to be shared.[2]

There was a marked difference between the response to NCBI processes from young people and that of adults, particularly teachers. Many younger people responded eagerly to the work. The teachers were more resistant, and this resistance centred around emotional healing. It was specifically the "speak out" - a point in the NCBI process where volunteers share a painful time of having been discriminated against which had the most profound - and sometimes disturbing - effect on some of the rest of the participants. This resistance, of teachers in particular to NCBI workshops led by the QPEP team, took the form of criticisms of it being 'very American.....(and)....the exercises around emotional healing were too public"[3] In my own dissertation, a report of one particular workshop included reactions to speak outs, describing them as "dangerous" and "needing professional guidance".[4] NCBI has had to deal with myths surrounding its work, one of which is that emotions are dangerous; one of NCBI's key assumptions is that emotions are not dangerous, it is unhealed and "unlistened to" emotions that are dangerous.

Other teachers interviewed as part of the external evaluation "did get quite a lot out of (the NCBI model) when used in an adult setting".[5] Several teachers became active members of NCBI N Ireland. However one of the findings of the external evaluation of QPEP was that "there was unease about the heavy reliance on the NCBI model, on its relevance to Northern Ireland and the sensitivities needed to handle some of its techniques."[6] In assessing its relevance to N Ireland it is important to understand the context.

The 1980's were a time when a number of conflict resolution models were being introduced to Northern Ireland, from the United States of America. McAllister makes the general point, that within Northern Ireland "there was a growing sense of the limitations of (any).... model that was 'mid Atlantic'."[7] This led to an attempt to 'inculturate' models, however as McAllister goes on to point out "within ourselves we still retained a sense that the 'American model' was best and that our task was to find Northern Irish clothes for it".[8]

The work of Jean Paul Lederach was beginning to influence conflict resolution practitioners in the early 1990's. He maintained that the key question was really about the cultural assumptions that exist in any North

American model. He acknowledged that

> embedded subtly in my training project was the unintended
> residue of imperialism. While hard to admit and even more
> difficult to recognise the outcome was clear to those who had eyes
> to see. The cultural assumptions of my context were moved to (a
> Central American context) with the underlying premise that mine
> were the right way to go and that they should learn it[9]

Lederach in his "Preparing for Peace" discusses the relative merits of prescriptive and elicitive approaches. He identifies the prescriptive approach as a "how to" approach where the trainer is the expert and learning and mastering the model is the primary goal of the event.

The elicitive approach has an emphasis that is "not only on empowerment as participation in creating models, but also in seeking resource and root in the cultural context itself."[10] Lederach acknowledges that there is a spectrum of approaches between purely elicitive and purely prescriptive.

The NCBI prejudice reduction process was prescriptive and designed to be replicable. NCBI was attempting to respond to the urgency of issues in many parts of the world that was requiring the training of a large number of leaders as quickly as possible. NCBI understood that there were things to lose and things to gain by having a replicable model. It had been developed over many years of practice, and in diverse settings. It was NCBI's experience that that it was least likely to get into difficulties and confrontations, given the highly charge emotional nature of these issues when people could be trained in a replicable model.

In NCBI's notes for trainers the point is made that,

> Various models have been designed to work with people from
> different backgrounds on eliminating prejudice. What has been
> missing, however is a systematic method, with clearly articulated
> assumptions, that can be easily be adapted in different settings.
> The following model has been implemented (widely)...and can be
> adjusted to meet the needs of different age groups, constituencies,

and organisations".[11]

However in Lederach's terms this still meant a "How to" approach. The NCBI N Ireland's struggle initially was how to establish a model that was replicable, keep its integrity and, yet be flexible enough to allow for the creativity of a local leadership. NCBI International saw the workshop as a "hook" to get people involved, with the ultimate goal of building teams of leaders across ethnic backgrounds, a goal that it clearly achieved among its National Associates.

NCBI International upholds the universality of the need for leaders to do emotional healing work in highly charged conflict areas. During the period 1988-93 over 150 people participated in Training the Trainer weekends in N Ireland led by Cherie Brown, including - for example - a majority of the key staff at the Northern Ireland Community Relations Council. The size of NCBI N Ireland, (made up of a team committed to leading prejudice reduciton work), did not reflect these numbers, as it fluctuated between 6 and 17 members.

The context in which those Training the Trainer weekends were happening helps make sense of the gap between the numbers who were trained to lead NCBI workshops, and those who subsequently joined NCBI N Ireland.

The Training the Trainer weekends became an annual tradition at a time when the number of individuals and agencies in the broad field of community relations training was increasing dramatically in Northern Ireland . At that time a number of initiatives were taking place in the sphere of anti-sectarian work (Workers Education Association, Irish Congress of Trade Unions, National Union of Students), anti-discrimina-tory practice (University of Ulster, Rupert Stanley College) and generally in prejudice reduction work (Protestant and Catholic Encounter [PACE], Co-Operation North) . They evolved from an expressed need to tackle problems, and were often supported by Government agencies like the Central Community Relations Unit (CCRU) or the Community Relations Council.

These initiatives illustrated that the time was ripe for prejudice reduc-tion work. It could be argued that people were only looking for exercises and models to add to their repertoire rather than becoming part of an ongoing team - NCBI N Ireland. Individuals might become involved in a follow-up meeting immediately after a Training the Trainer weekend, but membership of NCBI N Ireland reduced to a core as the year progressed. Looking back it became clear that NCBI N Ireland made the mistake of reinforcing this trend by giving higher priority to recruiting people for the Training the Trainer weekend as the major NCBI event of the year, rather than leading the workshops and building the team itself. Subsequently NCBI International has realised that in its chapters throughout the world, there is a need to shift the emphasis from Training the Trainer events, to developing its chapters.

Some difficulties which arose in the annual NCBI workshops were due to lack of clarity as to whether their purpose was to offer training in leadership of the model, or an in depth "taster" of the NCBI process. In planning for the 1993 Training for Trainers weekend, NCBI N Ireland were aware, that potential participants might only be looking for tools and techniques.

Among these difficulties were those that would be common to any process involving emotional healing. A prerequisite for would-be trainers in this field is their agreement to engage in their own emotional healing. Workshop participants who come with the sole objective of picking up new skills (to complement their existing repertoire) tend to resist such requirements.

Since emotional healing is an integral part of a Training the Trainer weekend, conscious efforts were made to specify this in the advance literature for the 1993 weekend. With hindsight, NCBI N Ireland should have ensured that all participants had some understanding of the nature of emotional healing, through experiencing a taster workshop. Because this was not done there was growing disquiet during the weekend amongst some of the participants about the process they were expected to be part of. For some it was a case of not being clear whether "this was meant to be an experiential workshop for participants to deal with their own deep-seated prejudices or a workshop to pass on skills"[12]; others expressed the need for "more time to assess and process the new information and methods they are encountering"[13]

The experience of the 1993 workshop in particular, clearly indicated that participants who are having their first experience of an NCBI workshop cannot be regarded as leaders undergoing training. Their decision for or against such a role must await reflection on the workshop experience.

The leaders on the 1993 Training the Trainer workshop did their best to balance the need to respond to resistance, with the need to train people who had come on the weekend expecting to be trained. The support group leaders were encouraged to put a time-limit on dealing with questions, and then to continue with the task. For some of the participants the issue was not *either* dealing with the questions *or* getting on with the task, there was a need to have more space for people to critically evaluate what they are encountering. (There was a) need to encourage scepticism.......welcome negative remarks as indicating that people were using their thinking and not swallowing this model wholesale.[15]

In 1993 NCBI had started to put in place a support structure using "empowerment people" whose role it was to assist participants to get things right for themselves. Due to the relatively small numbers of NCBI N Ireland leaders on the weekend, and the increased need for them to meet at break and lunchtime together, the NCBI N Ireland empowerment people were generally inaccessible to the very people they were trying to help. A lesson learned from that experience was the need for these empowerment people in highly charged emotional situations to be more available to participants.

For people already aware of the complementary relationship between the affective and cognitive domains, NCBI processes were "user friendly". Others identified with the need for more time and emotional support to digest the experience.

The cultural context has to be taken into consideration in explaining the resistance to the NCBI model. McLachlan would argue that in Northern Ireland there are cultural differences in the expression of emotion, both in public and private, depending on religious traditions.[16] In brief the public expression of emotion, and communal support is stronger amongst Catholics than Protestants. Most importantly, the province's recent history has a profound impact on any process which involves emotional healing.

A hypothesis that supports this perspective is that for the twenty five years up until the ceasefires in Autumn 1994, Northern Ireland was a province that had undergone massive population shifts, had experienced 3200 deaths, several thousand injuries, bombings, and continues to be a state whose law is enforced by emergency powers. Nevertheless the image of the mother pushing her pram, carrying her shopping and struggling to keep control of her children, whilst rioters and police fight in the street has become an icon of the Troubles. It symbolises normality within abnormality, and life going on as usual. In a community of only 1.5 million people, where 1 in 500 people have died as a result of the troubles, pain, grief and anger are just below the surface. Wilson posits that often these emotions are kept in place by politeness; by a "silent agreement not to touch on taboo subjects".[17]

However beneath this veneer of politeness there is often a great deal of resistance to any work requiring the emotions. Farrell argues that historically resistance is a way that people in Ireland have responded to "the being on the receiving end of other people's answers".[18] This resistance can be motivated by a demand to be more involved in a dialogue; or it can be borne out of the experience of past mistreatment, and of colonialism, and of prejudice itself.

It was a recurring facet of workshops that when asked how their lives had been touched by the Troubles, young people would respond that they had had no experience of them. Yet these would often be young people who were perceived as "knowing nothing else". One person's memory would spark off someone else's story, and these stories would engender feelings of horror or sadness that would often surprise the teller. What was at times a "taken for granted" event of family history, a familiar tale, would shock those who heard it for the first time.

This familiarity sometimes led to a denial, a denial of experience, and event of family history, a familiar tale, would shock those who heard it for the first time.

This familiarity sometimes led to a denial, a denial of experience, and the feelings associated with it, which in turn led to a denial of people's biography. Wilson coined the phrase "personal biography"[19] to illustrate that practitioners in particular are often found to be motivated by profound or significant events in their lives to become involved in community relations work. Their involvement may be based on an emotional decision as well as a rational one. Trainers are not mere technicians, although there is a temptation to seek skills without wishing to make an emotional investment. We each come to this work with something of ourselves invested in it. The transfer of skills in prejudice reduction inevitably involves each person learning from reflection on his/her own life , about the emotions that get attached to hurtful experiences, in themselves and others. Having recognised the existence of emotional hurts, the reducing of prejudice involves "emotional healing" which is a key part of the NCBI model. One of the key contributions of NCBI to work in N Ireland has been an understanding of the theory of *internalised oppression* . Namely that groups who have been historically oppressed can internalise that oppression and take it out on one another

There is a growing awareness in N Ireland of a need for communal healing, forgiveness and reconciliation, particularly since the ceasefires. For example in an article entitled "Weaving the Future Story" , Gorman proposes a "place of witness" where people can tell their stories, in a process of communal healing.[20]

The 1993 Training the Trainer weekend illustrated the need for NCBI N Ireland to be more pro-active in selecting potential participants for the weekend. Nevertheless there was a consistency in the resistance to NCBI processes which was only beginning to be acknowledged by NCBI N Ireland.

As National Associate I was used to feedback (often from people who had no direct experience of NCBI workshops), that they were "too American", "too confrontational" etc. I found the latter ironic as what had attracted me to NCBI in the first place was the fact that it was non-confrontational. Individuals didn't get targetted for who they were, for example.

Specifically I came to NCBI from 15 years of working for a children's holiday charity, where training volunteers from both traditions meant creating a co-operative atmosphere where people could make friends across the so called "sectarian divide" during the course of a weekend others opposing views but retreated from the idea for fear of upsetting their new found friendships. One particular wellmeaning attempt to do so had ended up in confrontations. Consequently I appreciated the methodology of NCBI which welcomed diversity, and encouraged particpants to take pride in who they were, but to respect differences.

A prescriptive model, needing to be replicable is not as responsive to the need for change as an elicitive one. A continuing challenge for NCBI is to allow for individual creativity, and cultural diversity in the style and delivery of workshops, whilst maintaining the integrity and the *replicability* of the model.

It is important to separate legitimate questioning from prejudice. While there may be validity in the often expressed concern that the NCBI model is "too American", this factor would seem less significant than the widespread resistance to emotional healing, (which is also experienced by NCBI leaders in the USA) and the prescriptive nature of the NCBI models.

Amongst members of NCBI N Ireland there is an awareness of the effectiveness of NCBI models. Part of this effecitiveness is the degree to which it is replicable, ie prescriptive. Yet NCBI N Ireland is also aware of the need for a more elicitive approach in N Ireland. An elicitive model, Lederach would argue, builds on the culture. It wouldn't *just take it into consideration* but would be borne out of the knowledge and wisdom, the pain and suffering and joy of a community or communities at war. This "shared and accumulated knowledge" would form an integral part of the process. The now prescriptive NCBI models have evolved via an elicitive process, through the collective experience of NCBI National Associates. NCBI leaders are encouraged to "own" the model and to develop their leadership. A contentious issue has been the fact that the NCBI Trainer's Notes are copyright. This issue is based on different perceptions of copyright on either side of the Atlantic. (In the UK it is often understood to mean "intellectual property", in the USA it is a legal requirement).

If, as Lederach suggests, there is often unaware US imperialism inherent in US models; this needs to be addressed, but in a way that doesn't attach blame, or feed into anti-US prejudice, or Irish internalised oppression.

In Northern Ireland, the prescriptive nature of the NCBI processes imposes considerable constraint on an individual leader's efforts both to use her/his personal creativity and to adapt the process to fit the cultural context and circumstances of a particular workshop.

The understandable tension for leaders between being encouraged to make the NCBI process their "own", and the need to preserve the integrity of those processes, was a continual one. Ownership can be understood to imply the right of trainers, using their "personal creativity and dynamic intelligence"[22] to adapt the process for the cultural context of the specific workshops.

This begs the question as to whether "owning" *a prescriptive* process. can mean anything other than "making your own the knowledge of the expert"[21]

As QPEP Director, I was in charge of an action research project. Action research is a circular process - identifying problems, trying out strategies, refining them, etc, essentially encouraging an elicitive approach. I was faced with a challenge as NCBI National Associate and was meeting resistance in promoting a prescriptive model. Resistance being a recurring problem, it lent itself to an action-research approach to its resolution. In order to deal with the resistance it was necessary to "listen" to the feedback, to try and sort out prejudice from clear thinking, and to learn lessons. A great deal was learnt from the 1993 week, that has been described in this chapter and it led to members of NCBI N Ireland taking stock. For a period of three months they met weekly to read through the manual, to reflect on their experience of leading it, and to practice alternative ways of delivering it.

By 1994, NCBI N Ireland was reduced to a nucleus of five or six people. At a time of burgeoning interest in anti-sectarian work, such as the dynamic Irish Congress of Trades Unions (ICTU) initiative "Counteract" and the initiatives already mentioned, the impact of NCBI has been diffuse and intangible, but none the less influential for that. Prior to the first NCBI Training the Training "Prejudice Reduction" Weekend, the very term *prejudice reduction* was relatively unknown. NCBI workshops have helped it become part of the community relations vocabulary.

The Ulster Quaker Peace Education Project had a major role in developing the work of NCBI N Ireland. McAllister identifies four key stages of development in incorporating models from outside N Ireland - Importation, Inculturation, Indigenisation and finality Mutuality. It is this fourth stage that NCBI N Ireland is currently entering into. It has to use assistance from outside in a "carefully managed strategic way" in order to encourage the "fuller emergence of indigenous knowledge....and communal wisdom"[22], whilst taking advantage of the collective experience represented by the NCBI processes.

There is anecdotal evidence from individual workshops that participating in NCBI processes has had a profound positive impact on people's understanding. An example of this is in a survey of the participants of three workshops in 1990 which indicated, even when there were difficulties with the emotional healing aspects, the workshops did lead to a greater understanding of the nature of prejudice [?]. There is little doubt that the experience has transformed attitudes, and possibly led to changed behaviour. Even on the 1993 workshop there was recognition that the aim in terms of creating awareness of the nature of prejudice had been achieved.

Work has yet to be done to create sufficient places of safety and mutual respect, where people can be comfortable enough to risk feeling uncomfortable; and take responsibility for being witness, albeit belatedly, to the emotional healing that will help create the energy to truly welcome diversity and build alliances between traditionally opposed groups.

There is no ready made formula for fusing the collective wisdom that is born from the widespread experience of indigenous diversity work in Northern Ireland with the profound, transforming essence of the NCBI processes. The initiative has to come from within N Ireland, and in partnership with NCBI International there is likely to be a new beginning This process of learning how to become allies towards a common goal is itself transforming.

NOTES

1. Pegg, Will (1990) "Prejudice Reduction - A Workshop Approach" QPEP, Derry (1990)
2. McKittrick, David (1992) p35 "PACE - A Field Officer's Perspective", PACE Volume 24 No. 1.
3. O'Neill, Jim (1993) . Para 4.8.3 "Quaker Peace Education Project Evaluation - Final Report", Charities Evaluation Services Belfast,

4. Tyrrell, Jerry (1991) "The NCBI Prejudice Reduction Model and Teachers' Resistance in N.Ireland" MA dissertation. University of Ulster. March 1991.
5. O'Neill, Jim (1993) Ibid Para 4.8.3
6. O'Neill, Jim (1993) Ibid Para 1.2.3
7. McAllister, Brendan (1994) "Mediation and the Northern Ireland Conflict" - a paper. Mediation Network for Northern Ireland.
8. Ibid.
9. Lederach, Jean Paul (1995) "Preparing for Peace - Conflict Tran formation across Cultures" Syracuse University Press, Syracuse, New York.
10. Lederach, Jean Paul (1995) Ibid.
11. Brown, Cherie R, 'Prejudice Reduction Workshops', Notes for trainers, Mimeograph,(1988)
12. Tyrrell, Jerry (1993) "NCBI Welcoming Diversity Training Week end - June 1993". Evaluation for the NICommunity Relations Council. .
13. Ibid.
14. Tyrrell, Jerry (1993) Ibid.
15. Ibid.
16. McLachlan , Peter, (1994) Transcript of Interview by Jerry Tyrrell, Belfast. May 1994
17. Wilson, Derick (1994) in "The EMU Promoting School" Conference Report, University of Ulster, 1994
18. Farrell, Seamus (1995) Unpublished paper.
19. Wilson, Derick (1992) speech Newcastle, Co Down. May 1992
20. Gorman, Damian (1994) "Weaving the Future Story" A mimeograph. N. Ireland. November 1994
21. Lederach, Jean Paul (1995) Ibid.
22. McAllister, Brendan (1994) Ibid.

CHAPTER 15: THE CHARITIES EVALUATION SERV-ICES (CES) EVALUATION OF THE ULSTER QUAKER PEACE EDUCATION PROJECT

This chapter describes the setting up of the evaluation, identifies issues contained in it, and examines how QPEP responded to the recommendations.

The setting up of the external evaluation

In June 1992 the QPEP Management Committee decided that an external evaluation of the project was needed in "anticipation of Government proposals over what funding would be available for voluntary projects"[1], in the future. The Committee also wanted to

> confirm with the Dept of Education , N Ireland (DENI) that (the evaluation) we would like to arrange to have done is what they would like to see from an external point of view.[2]

The following month the Management Committee chairperson and I met with Clem McCartney and as a result of this meeting an outline evaluation proposal was drawn up.[3]

This outline proposal identified the task, research structure, method of evaluation, cost and source of funding. The task boiled down to a descriptive evaluation of current practice, and evaluation of the Project's impact, and possibilities of development.

The anticipated research structure was an independent evaluation, with support and supervision of research by the Centre for the Study of Conflict, and active preconsultation with DENI. The intended method would involve participant observation; evaluative discussions with the QPEP team; structured interviews with staff, volunteers and Management Committee members, and with teachers and others. Finally it was anticipated that there would be discussion with relevant agencies in the field of EMU. Originally a budget of £15,000 for the evaluation was mooted, with funding coming from Charitable Trusts and DENI.

In the next six months approaches were made to potential funders, and discussions entered into with the Charities Evaluation Services (CES).

CES had a set of guiding principles which fitted in with QPEP's approach.

> A guarantee of confidentiality and ownership by the commis-
> sioning agent; an action-research approach which feeds results
> into the everyday practice of organisations in order to contribute
> to their development; an incorporation of self-evaluation meth-
> ods and user participation; a commitment to quality assurance;
> and an attempt to abide by our equal opportunities policy [4]

The initial evaluation proposal from CES [5] acknowledged the joint management of QPEP, its active use of volunteers, the involvement of teachers in workshops, and the variety of areas of work.

It stressed that there would be substantial consultation

> to ensure that the evaluation does justice to the work of this
> important project in the context of the increasing attention being
> paid to community relations and in the light of the substantial
> credibility provided by the project's parentage, and the relevance
> of the project to government educational policy [6]

The original CES estimate was £16,000. Three potential funders had been identified, DENI, the Joseph Rowntree Charitable Trust , and a Quaker legacy - the Jessie Cairns bequest. DENI after initial interest was unable to support the evaluation financially. The evaluation proposal was modified after consultation with QPEP and potential funders.

The Joseph Rowntree Charitable Trust expressed concern about the number of consultancy days involved, and

> the balance between resources allocated to looking at documents
> and talking to stake holders and resources allocated to looking at
> impact and considering the strategy for the future.[7]

For the Trust the key issue was one of impact, and they felt that the emphasis was weighted too much in the direction of analysing the history of the project.

The overall budget had now be cut to £10,000. A second proposal was drafted by the Charities Evaluation Services, which took into account suggested changes. Savings were also made by QPEP agreeing to provide a placement student to assist the evaluator.

The Jessie Cairns Bequest was concerned about the overall cost of the project, and had a suggestion regarding discussion with stake-holders, "that the idea of consulting people by telephone should be avoided if at all possible"[8]

The third and final evaluation proposal, which formed part of the contract, was constrained by the need to keep within a budget of £5,000. This was funded by the Joseph Rowntree Charitable Trust and the Jessie Cairns Bequest. Jim O'Neill was appointed by CES as an evaluator and started work on 1st June 1993.

The original intention of involving a student on placement in the evaluation had to be abandoned due to the late start . Seamus Farrell provided assistance by transcribing the tapes of interviews.

An advisory support group was set up, consisting of Richard Holmes (DENI), Felicity McCartney (Joseph Rowntree Charitable Trust; Jessie Cairns Bequest), Alan Pearson (Ulster Quaker Peace Committee) and Jerry Tyrrell (QPEP). This group met three times.

Jim O'Neill presented a draft evaluation report to the QPEP Management Committee in October 1993, and after receiving comments submitted the final evaluation report in December 1993.

Issues raised by the evaluation

Acknowledging that "QPEP has been recognised as providing a valuable service both to schools and other agencies" [9], O'Neill concluded however that there was little prioritising and limited development of strategies. At times QPEP did take the initiative and approach schools. However there was little strategic planning and as Farrell points out

> while the project is commended for it responsiveness to individual requests from schools and other agencies, the (CES Evaluation) Report found that this led to its being over-extended and reactive rather than pro-active.[10]

A contentious issue was O'Neill's conclusion that "a lot of energy and resources were put into the work with other agencies which could have been better utilised in working more with schools".[11] As a general rule work with other agencies - which was by and large adult education work - was at weekends. Nonetheless the planning and administration of these was done during the week. It could be argued that this focussed attention away from work with schools. Nevertheless QPEP's aims in the second phase included developing work with other agencies. What the CES Evaluation consistently managed to do was to point out areas which could have benefited from prioritisation.

The conclusion that

> not enough ongoing evaluation was carried out within QPEP which could have provided more self-critical analysis and help set priorities.[12]

did reflect a growing concern amongst staff and volunteers. As Farrell pointed out

> what I consider most useful in the Evaluation Report is its findings with regard to ongoing reflection and evaluation within the project and its strong recommendations about these for the future[13]

With three evaluation weekends throughout the life of the project, and a process of continual evaluation of workshops, evaluation data was available. However the project was "workshop driven", and time needed to be set aside to reflect on the learnings from evaluations. Insufficient time was created for this, and at times mistakes were repeated, or there wasn't the time to try out new ideas and approaches, depending instead on tried and tested ones.

The role of the Management Committee came in for some criticism. O'Neill made the point that "it should have been more clearly defined in its dealings with staff. Better channels of communication could have helped deal earlier with a particular conflict which arose."[14]

Throughout the six years of the project, membership of the Management Committee remained the same, with the exception of John Darby who was replaced by Seamus Dunn as the Director of the Centre for the Study of Conflict. It was set up to manage a project involving one full time member of staff, employed by the University. In 1991 when additional full time paid staff were appointed directly by QPEP, the new role of the committee as employers was not spelt out to the committee. The fact that QPEP evolved into a project using a pool of a dozen or more volunteers and three full-time staff gave it the role of a voluntary organisation working with different client groups, whereas it continued to be structured within the University as if it were a one person project. The CES evaluation pointed up the need for a successor project to have a Management Committee that "reflects its user groups. The channels of supervision and accountability should be made clear to reduce the potential for conflict" [15]

Throughout its life QPEP had existed on a day to day basis with informal procedures between staff and volunteers, with few arrangements for selection and recruitment, and no formal grievance or disciplinary procedures, for volunteers. This informal working environment contained few checks and balances for dealing with conflict. The high level of expectations of communication, co-operation and affirmation, and the consensus approach of a workshop was sometimes at odds with the reality of the working relationships in the inevitable hierarchy of the project itself.

Nevertheless, writing in QPEP's final annual report, O'Neill commented that

> What struck me most in the process of carrying out this evaluation was the amount of goodwill that existed among many of the client groups towards QPEP. There was a genuine desire that the work of the organisation should continue in whatever form. [16]

It was this feedback, summarised in the first of the Evaluation's recommendations that renewed the Management Committee's determination for the work to continue.

The recommendations all of which are printed here, were acted on as follows:

Recommendations of the Charities Evaluation Services Evaluation Report of the Ulster Quaker Peace Education Project.[17]

7.1.   The work that the project has developed in the fields of conflict resolution and prejudice reduction should be continued.

This helped galvanise the project to explore potential structures for supporting future work. The particular prejudice reduction work of QPEP had been developed in conjunction with NCBI N Ireland. The impending demise of QPEP provided a useful moment for the two agencies to disengage, with NCBI N Ireland already being a separate entity.

7.2   It is recommended that everyone involved with QPEP including the Management Committee, staff and volunteers come together to discuss the way forward for the project. It is vital that strategic plans are formulated by them in order to allow funding applications to be submitted and processed before the end of the present project's lifespan.

In January 1994 QPEP organised a day whereby eight people comprising members of staff, volunteers and management committee members met to discuss future work, based on a reading of the Evaluation Report. The outcome of the day reflected the overall recommendations of the CES evaluation, including a future project being led by strategy rather than demand; taking on board different processes/activities and being flexible in their use while locating them in the local culture.

Later the same month a seminar was organised, involving the Management Committee, and individuals from outside agencies, the Northern Ireland Curriculum Council; the Centre for the Study of Conflict; teachers; the Western Education and Library Board, Jim O'Neill (the CES evaluator) and a representative of Ireland Yearly meeting of the Society of Friends (Quakers). Taking into account the outcome of the previous internal discussions of QPEP, those present at the seminar came up with

a series of issues that needed to be addressed in planning a successor to QPEP. Clarity was needed in spelling out the relationship between the future project and the education system in general.[18]

It would need to be demonstrably linked to the curriculum. There was a consensus that it would be best to be part of the Centre for the Study of Conflict.

The seminar ended by drawing up a broad action plan and working party was set up to start drafting a funding proposal to DENI. The title of the new project was "The EMU Promoting School"

7.3   It is recommended that funding is sought to continue the work

Up until the end of QPEP in December 1994, the funding was the responsibility of the Ulster Quaker Peace Committee (UQPC). UQPC had been consistent in viewing its role as an initial funder, up to a maximum of six years. A future project would require a new sponsor.

In April 1994 the process was set in motion to establish a charitable trust - the Positive Ethos Trust - to sponsor the EMU Promoting School Project. Individuals with active involvement in education as teachers, curriculum officers, researchers, field officers and others with an interest in mediation and evaluation were invited to become trustees. Legal advice was sought to get the new trust registered with the Inland Revenue.

7.4   It is recommended that contracting options with the forthcoming United Nations University INCORE programme be explored. QPEP has already made contact with this body and this should be followed up and pursued to develop joint work with INCORE.

QPEP was an action research project with the Centre for the Study of Conflict. The Centre had been instrumental in the negotiations between the University of Ulster and the United Nations University that created INCORE. During the feasibility study that led to the establishment of INCORE (The INitiative on COnflict Resolution and Ethnicity), a visiting panel had participated in workshops with children, organised by QPEP. It is too early to specify what links, if any, could be established between INCORE and any body that replaced QPEP.

7.6   If a future project decides to concentrate its work in schools it is recommended that it negotiate with the Western Education and Library Board for a teacher secondment. This will allow easier access to in-service course provision for teachers.

7.7   It is recommended that the production of educational packages which are more readily usable by teachers of EMU be given priority by the project.

This recommendation was to have the most profound effect in terms of staffing. The Positive Ethos Trust was to take on the recommendation, in all its applications for funding.

If a teacher was employed as a field officer it would help to focus a future project on the needs to root the programmes in the classroom experience, with particular reference to materials and resources. It was clear from the experience of EMU co-ordinators in schools, that they often felt isolated amongst their own staff. A field officer who was a teacher would be more likely to understand the dynamics of a school, and empathise with a teacher who was having to deal with resistance, and offer practical support, for example. S/he would also be sympathetic to staff who felt that innovations were an imposition; and would be aware of what was effective in educational packages, and what was not.

7.8 It is recommended that any organisation that follows QPEP should adapt on-going self-evaluation. This would allow the organisation to monitor the achievement of targets and set priorities.

As indicated in a previous chapter, there were opportunities for evaluation throughout the project, but not in a structured way that assisted the development of a strategic plan. During the latter stages of the project, the work benefited from the single minded work of individuals who were prepared to apply the benefits of their research to improve the practice. This rigour was particularly beneficial to the project during the course of the Peer Mediation programme - (see Chapter 16).

During the course of setting up the new EMU Promoting School Project, it became clear that undertaking such high quality research and setting up structures for self-evaluation needed to be the responsibility of an individual worker. Funding was sought to employ a research assistant.

7.9 In the event that it is decided to develop a successor project, it is recommended that a Management Committee is set up which reflects its user-groups. The channels of supervision and accountability should be made clear to reduce the potential for conflict. Possible members should be identified as soon as possible. Their immediate task will be to establish the aims and objectives of the successor project and explore funding opportunities.

The "immediate task" referred to above was taken on by a working party set up to draft a proposal to DENI, and the Central Council for Examinations and Assessment (CCEA) for funding. As previously mentioned the Positive Ethos Trust was set up later in 1994, only one of whose members had been directly involved in QPEP; the others reflected the sort of user group QPEP had worked with. The Trustees effectively were the Management Committee from the establishment of the Trust in August 1994 until early 1995. The contract that was drawn up between the University of Ulster and the Positive Ethos Trust, for the EMU Promoting School project, was based on a number of the recommendations regarding management- particularly t the need for clear channels of supervision.

The CES evaluation formed the basis of the discussions that led to the establishment of a new action research project, which by January 1995 had two full-time staff appointed. The final chapter sums up the developments of QPEP and points to the expected focus of the new project.

NOTES
1. Boyd, Felicity (1992) Minutes of Management Committee, QPEP
2. Ibid.
3. Lampen, John (1992) QPEP - Outline Evaluation Proposal , 1992
4. McGinn, Pat (1993) Proposal to the QPEP for an Evaluation from Charities Evaluation Services, January 1993
5. Ibid.
6. Ibid.
7. Pittam, Stephen (1993) Letter to Jerry Tyrrell 10.3.93
8. Tennant, Peter (1993) Letter to Jerry Tyrrell, 26.3.93
9. O'Neill, Jim (1993) Para 1.3.1 Final Report, Quaker Peace Education Project Evaluation, Charities Evaluation Services, December 1993
10. Farrell, Seamus (1995) p54 QPEP Annual Report 1993-4, Jan 1995
11. O'Neill, Jim (1993) Ibid. Para 1.3.2
12. O'Neill, Jim (1993) Ibid. Para 1.3.4
13. Farrell, Seamus (1995) Ibid.
14. O'Neill, Jim (1993) Ibid. Para 1.3.5
15. O'Neill, Jim (1993) Ibid. Para. 7.9
16. O'Neill, Jim (1995) p52 QPEP Annual Report 1993-4, January 1995.
17. O'Neill, Jim (1993) Ibid. Para 7
18. Tyrrell, Jerry (1995) p60 QPEP Annual Report 1993-4, January 1995

CHAPTER 16: THE PILOT PEER MEDIATION PROJECT

In September 1993, the Ulster Quaker Peace Education Project embarked on a pilot peer mediation project with two primary schools in Derry. At the same time the draft CES evaluation of QPEP was being produced, and some of the initial recommendations, particularly with reference to action-research were being made known. The Pilot Peer Mediation Project benefited from the learning involved.

From the outset, QPEP was aware of peer mediation programmes being developed in the USA. It was itself involved in 1989 in drafting a proposal to the Department of Education (N.Ireland) for the funding of a pilot peer mediation project.(5) Though considered sympathetically, funding was not forthcoming. This effectively brought initiatives to an end for three years until Mary de Largy''s major work in Belfast in 1991/2.[1].

QPEP's experience of using its conflict resolution skills model indicated that it had potential for further logical development in that these skills could be applied to training children in concrete skills of negotiation and mediation. In February 1993 the Project's staff and volunteers agreed to set up a peer mediation pilot project.[2]

Preliminary Stage

In 1993 it was decided to devote QPEP's annual P7 Conference to the theme of "Peer Mediation".[3] Participants observed a demonstration of mediation, and had an opportunity in role-plays, to try it for themselves. Some teaching in the basic techniques was offered. In addition a brochure entitled "Conflict Busters"[4] was distributed.

The Principals of the Model Primary School and Oakgrove Integrated Primary School responded positively to a subsequent invitation to all Londonderry primary schools to participate in a pilot peer mediation project. One Principal in particular was influenced by the enthusiastic feedback provided by his school's delegates to the P7 conference .

Research Instruments for Training Component

Using Elliott's definition of action/research as "the study of a social situation with a view to improving the quality of action within it",[5] QPEP had as its immediate research objective the development of a process which would inform the action - specifically the training of children in mediation skills. After each workshop the children's evaluations were collated into a usable form for the planning of the next one. As the workshops progressed, the questions in these forms enabled the facilitators to obtain indications as to the learning acquired, 'gaps' in the learning, and the needs of participants. Classroom work, for each of the periods between workshops, was examined and fed back into subsequent planning.

Regular contact was maintained with the teachers, and with the Principals, as well as a formal meeting to review the training and discuss the establishment of the mediation programme in their schools.

For a pilot project of this nature the provision of parallel initial training for an entire P7 class in each of two schools, had numerous advantages. Both were 'ideal' schools in many respects. QPEP had already established a good working relationship with both schools.

A vital objective of the project was to demonstrate that peer mediation can work, Another was to identify what would be required of a prospective school in terms of commitment from Principal and Staff, before attempting it there. It needs to be stressed that neither Principal had heard of peer mediation in schools before.

The Team and Team Training

Most of the QPEP team were experienced in using QPEP's workshop model for the development of affirmation, communication and cooperation skills. However the team's first Training Day began with quite frank acknowledgements of scepticism as to the feasibility of peer mediation and of personal doubts as regards competence. Fortunately, one team member with considerable mediation training experience was available to lead the training sessions. Handbooks and training schemes from other projects were useful resources. Input on the first Team Training Day on the basic format of mediation processes was helpful as a structure from which to develop a process for use by children.

The childrens' training programme - of six 105 minutes workshops to take place once per week in each school between October and December 1993 - was devised. An overall course syllabus to fit this schedule was drawn up.

The format of the training sessions of the QPEP team consisted of team members 'doing' the kinds of exercises which were being envisaged for the children. Then through analysis and evaluation, the team designed the exercise for use in the childrens' workshops. Trialling in the use of fairy stories as the basis of role-plays indicated that they could be very effective indeed in seeing the same incident from two perspectives.

As the childrens' workshops progressed, a number of dilemmas surfaced and were addressed in team training and planning, including the fact that childrens' mediation does not mirror adult practice. Children are more concerned with restoring friendship - or at least peaceful coexistence - than with tying up all the issues in a formal agreement.

Continued evidence of the children's innate skill and intuition indicated that the team's primary challenge was to trust the children to find their way of proceeding. It was also crucial to convey to the children that the common conflicts of school life would be treated seriously, rather than being minimised by the grown-up world.

The Workshops

The workshops taught mediation skills in the context of the themes of affirmation, communication and cooperation. The P7 teacher in each school played one of the roles in "The Old Woman and the Woodcutter" conflict (the Hansel and Gretel story), in the first round of workshops. The exercise, though well-prepared, was deliberately unrehearsed in terms of final outcome and came across as very real. Evidence of children's interest came quickly.

The children were soon involved in role-playing the conflicting parties, with the mediation roles played by a QPEP facilitator assisted by another child. All the children were then involved in the development of ideas as to how the mediators might proceed.

As the workshops progressed the childrens' participation expanded. The small group format was increasingly used so that each child would have opportunities to practise being mediators. At the final workshop actual conflicts (involving children who were present) were mediated; this led to a particularly popular workshop.

The evaluations and feedback of the six workshops indicated gaps in the training and other needs. These included the need to establish that the parties were taking part in mediation by choice, the distinction between mediation and arbitration, more practice for the children in framing the issues, and further exploration of the range of techniques for finding solutions to problems. These issues were addressed in the joint training day that had been planned from the beginning. .

Classwork indicated an excellent level of understanding overall and also of motivation, including a distinct preference for peer mediation above having teachers or parents involved. The importance of "keeping secrets" and the significance of resolution being achieved by the conflicting parties, were acknowledged by the children. The children at both schools recognised the need for mediators to have trust, honesty, fairness, listening skills, patience, confidentiality, and helpfulness.

All but three of the children in both schools agreed that they would like to see a peer mediation project in their schools. However the final question, as regards possible problems with a mediation programme, indicated impressive realism on the part of the children.

Establishment of a Peer Mediation Service

Each school was keen to establish the service, with 12 to 15 children functioning as mediators on a rota system. Both schools had similar plans for the regular debriefing of mediators, and arrangements for the safe keeping of records, statistics and copies of agreements. It was agreed that peer mediation should not be compulsory and other avenues remained open to an aggrieved child.

Within the QPEP team there was concern around the process of selection of mediators. It related to the pattern in education of the "brightest and best" being selected, whether for grammar school or to represent the school in competitions, and the psychological effects on those (consistently) not selected. Both schools opted for a peer selection process, with minimal intervention by teachers, and for only those selected to participate in the joint training day.

Among those chosen as mediators there were a few whose behaviour had given cause for some concern. They proved excellent as mediators, and their behaviour improved noticeably. This suggested that the project had potential to significantly address issues of behavioural change, through encouragement of children who were regularly in and out of conflict, to be mediators. It has been borne out by experience in other parts of the world that successful peer mediation schemes depend on this 'poacher-turned-gamekeeper' factor. The P7 teachers and playground supervisors involved, in both schools expressed great enthusiasm for exploring the possibilities of the project in this area.

Research Instruments for Programme Implementation

It was considered important to ensure that what would be asked from the schools in respect of our research requirements would be kept to an absolute minimum. A prime consideration was that the nature of the project itself required special sensitivity since it touched on the school's discipline policy and practice, and current methods of dealing with conflicts. The confidentiality of mediation proceedings had been stressed in training and it was felt that adults sitting in on mediations would both confuse the children and be intrusive to the fledgling programme.

The research function operated in tandem with the on-going support which QPEP gave to the schools during the second and third terms. During the second last week of the school year, individual interviews were conducted with the Principal, the P7 Teacher and the Senior Playground Supervisor in each school.

Implementation of Peer Mediation programmes

In February 1994 the scheme was introduced at both schools. This was done through explanation, role-plays and responding to questions. It was noted that the mediators became progressively more competent in their presentations and grown-ups were impressed by how impressively they fielded questions.

At this stage P7 children were the most frequent users of the scheme - and the mediators among them were very willing indeed to use it for the resolution of their own conflicts. At one school the P7 class teacher was immediately impressed by the thoroughness and patience with which mediators exercised their role. He also noted the transfer of skills to other areas of the curriculum and of the quality of interactions in general in the classroom.

The mediators would be completing their primary education in June and both schools envisaged the programme continuing and becoming integral to the life of the school. The induction of the P6 children, who would inherit the mediation role in the following year, therefore required attention. QPEP facilitated workshops for all the P6 children in both schools during the last term.

From the beginning of the pilot project it became apparent that insufficient account had been taken of the crucial role of Lunchtime Supervisors; and that they ought to have been involved in the training programme and consulted during the planning of the schemes. Lunch and playtimes are major occasions of conflict and also appropriate times for the provision of a mediation service. These are also the periods when children are the responsibility of the Lunchtime Supervisors; their work gives them unique insights as regards individual children and the dynamics of relationships between them.

With minimal briefing on the programme while the training was in progress, it is significant that they became fully involved in the provision of the mediation services from the beginning. Those in charge of supervision in both schools expressed interest in participating in training in future and willingness to attend outside their working hours. Both women acknowledged their scepticism towards the idea on first hearing about it, yet became enthusiastic supporters of it on seeing it in operation.

The issue pointed up the fact that the establishment of a peer mediation programme opens up the entire field of whole-school relationships - between children and adults and among adults. As regards the latter it challenges conventional hierarchical structures based on the identification of the teaching role as being on a different level from that of other roles.

Review of the Programmes in the two schools

The programmes operated during the last two terms of the school year. The services of mediators began to be used quite quickly, particularly among the P7 children, but increasingly involving the P6 children at The Model. There was resistance however among the P6 children at Oakgrove, frequently expressed through faking conflicts for the fun of being mediated!

In both schools the P5 and P4 children gradually began to use the scheme. There was no conscious decision to exclude younger children, but rather a feeling that in the first year it would be best to see how it would work with the senior children. Their only contact with the programme in its first year was at the Assemblies at which it was introduced.

After the initial interest however the number of mediations requested decreased. A number of reasons for the lull were identified. The more time elapsed after the initial launching and introduction events, the more the programme got lost and forgotten about - a pointer to the need in future to maintain promotion. But a fundamental reason has to be the failure of the Project to involve the Lunchtime Supervisors right from the start.

Impetus was greatly restored to the programmes following the workshops for the P6 children. Though the focus of these was on the next school year, when the participants would become mediators, an immediate outcome was the number of mediations increasing, and this level was maintained until the end of the year. The workshops brought the P6 children 'on board' and they began to use the service as they had not done previously. It also gave their teachers direct experience of the programme for the first time. They were very positive indeed about it.

The Principals' end-of-year assessments were extremely positive as regards the increase in skills, confidence and competence of the children and the programme was found to have more than met their expectations for the first year. The P7 class teachers involved were of the opinion that playground incidents were reduced as a result of the programme. The Senior Lunchtime Supervisor was even more certain about its positive impact, pointing in particular to the unusual calmness in the concluding weeks of the school year, which are usually volatile.

Interviews with Children

Interviews with children, both mediators and mediated led to the conclusion that:-

> The one things that stands out is the commitment of the children - and teachers- to mediation. it became clear that they feel mediation is a great way for conflicts to be resolved. The fact that it is children mediating other children appeals to both the mediators and the mediated.[6]

The comments of adults in general about the maturity which the mediators demonstrated, relate to several factors. One was their ability to distinguish the conflicts that should be referred to the teachers. Another was their patience with the parties, a quality that was extensively tested. The childrens' use of their own initiative both in bringing conflicts to mediation and in their handling of difficult situations, was frequently evident.

The single biggest challenge identified by the mediators was to maintain neutrality in the context of the diversity of their relationships with various disputants. Several children had experience of being both mediator and mediated. From the interviews it was clear that though some admitted to feeling 'strange" whether in mediating a dispute involving a classmate or in being themselves mediated, they had coped well with such feelings.

There was a consensus among the interviewed children that they had learned a lot about conflict and had developed confidence in dealing with it. As one member of staff said: "We don't give children enough credit for what they can do; we really don't"[7]

Looking to the Future

For both teachers and principals there was complete agreement on the need for detailed planning of the year ahead. It would have to include components for promoting the involvement of ancillary staff and of teachers of children other than the Primary 7s. and raising awareness among parents and school board members. It would also include strategies for increasing the programme's accessibility and visibility, and not least to the younger children. Both schools were clear about the need for continued external agency help in the establishment of the programme.

The relationship of the programme to Education for Mutual Understanding (EMU) and to the N.Ireland context in general featured strongly in the reflections of principals and teachers. Both schools had a strong commitment to the promotion of EMU and were in the fore-front of the search for authentic ways of delivering it. Their enthusiasm for the peer-mediation programme related to its being a practical way of delivering EMU.

Feasibility

With one year of the pilot project completed, substantial evidence emerged to indicate that the concept of a peer mediation service in primary schools is indeed feasible, given certain conditions.

Immediate and long-term benefits

Apart from what it offers to children as preparation for life, it can be of real and immediate benefit to everyone who is part of the life of the school. Children are empowered to contribute to developing the happy environment which is so crucial for learning.

Education for living

Conflict is a recurrent reality in human encounters. The results of this pilot project argue for the recognition of 'conflict literacy' as an important component of education. When seen in this wider context it may be necessary in future to guard against mediation coming to be seen as a specialist skill, as the preserve of experts. It will be important to offer the training to all the children in a class or even a school, although only some may have the chance to function in the school's formal mediation service.

It will also be important to locate the programme more clearly in the context of all relationships within a school. It was a peer mediation programme - but of at least equal concern must be teacher-pupil relationships. There is a much greater power imbalance in these than is likely in peer relationships and teacher-pupil conflict (especially in secondary schools) may often be a much greater area of tension than inter-pupil conflict.

As a pilot, peer mediation project, in two primary schools, the project was small but it could contribute significantly to the process of developing mediation practice throughout the education system, embracing all in-school relationships, and feeding into the promotion of a conflict resolution culture in society.

Recommendations

1: That a peer mediation service be established in schools in N.Ireland.

2: That interested schools be made aware of what would be required of them and a negotiated contract signed by the school and any outside agency.

3: That as many children as possible be trained in each school; that appropriate procedures be developed for the selection of those who will function as mediators, and for those not selected to   have complementary functions in the service's provision.

4: That Northern Ireland based resources be developed.

5: The service's development crucially requires an action/re search process. Interested schools should be made aware of the research requirements of the agency. Contractual arrange ments in respect of these should be negotiated at the beginning.

6: That an external agency or agencies be established to assist schools in the development of recommendations 1-5 over the next five years (1995 - 1999).

NOTES

1. de Largy, Mary, M Ed dissertation. "An Investigation of Conflict Resolution as applied to an Inner City Girl's Secondary School", Queen's University, Belfast, 1992

2. Quiery, Marie. "Report on Residential Weekend, 5th-7th February 1993 Staff and Volunteers Evaluation, QPEP, 1993

3. QPEP Annual Report 1992-3 pp19-20.

4. Lampen J. Conflict Busters: The Young Peoples' Guide to Media tion in Schools, QPEP, University of Ulster April 1993

5. Elliott J. 1982 Action-Research: A framework for self-evaluation in schools. Working Paper No 1. Teacher-Pupil Interaction and the Quality of Learning. London Schools Council - mimeo),

6. Miller, Annette, (1994) "Peer Mediation Project" A report of the QPEP project at Oakgrove and Model Primary Schools, January-June 1994

7. Laverty, Kathy, (1994) Transcript of Interview by Jerry Tyrrell, Oakgrove Primary School, Derry, June 1994

CHAPTER 17: BUILDING ON FIRM FOUNDATIONS

This concluding chapter summarises the development of QPEP from an idea at a conference to a full-blown action research project; and points to the future direction of the work under the auspices of the EMU Promoting School project.

QPEP quickly found its niche in the tradition of experiential peace education projects, arguably being more at home in the mores of informal adult education, than in an academic institution. For example its work with life prisoners at Maghaberry prison stimulated and informed its work, and was one field where it was not perceived as preaching to the converted.

The initial emphasis on action rather than research, and interaction with teachers rather than developing curriculum materials, reflected the aspirations of those involved in setting up the project. It also suited the modus operandi of QPEP for pragmatic reasons, the first QPEP team being recruited and trained to run workshops rather than be researchers. Nevertheless in the context of Elliott's definition of action research, from the outset QPEP used evaluation as a means of action research; creating the potential for more focussed research. This too was in the tradition of experiential peace education, as epitomised by the Kingston Friends Workshop Group who had a seminal influence on QPEP. Experiential learning lends itself to action research, although it was argued that QPEP was workshop driven, and inadequate priority was given to reflecting on its action. Gaps in reflection were indicated when staff and volunteers became aware of mistakes being repeated, and workshop programmes being recycled instead of involving innovation. Nevertheless the regular use of undergraduates from the peace and conflict studies course, enhanced the research aspect of the project. More could have been done to reciprocate this, through greater involvement of QPEP in the delivery of the MA and BA.

The broad remit of trialling and developing untried strategies of peace education, gave QPEP scope to take risks, make mistakes and respond to requests. It had a key role in developing the work of NCBI in N Ireland. It worked in close collaboration with other agencies, notably PACE, Co-

Operation North, in the development of new approaches to existing programmes that addressed diversity issues. It helped to introduce Alternatives to Violence Project (AVP) to Northern Ireland. Above all it raised the debate about conflict resolution skills in education, and consistently heralded the underlying philosophy of affirmation, communication and co-operation.

Initially QPEP was such an unproven resource that it was only through existing links that individual staff had with schools that it could get into schools at all. The first phase, notable for the way in which the QPEP team of staff and volunteers were established, and the far reaching role they had, was an opportunity to create an abundance of expertise and experience in conflict resolution skills workshops. This coupled with a growing awareness of the unease that some teachers had for more interactive education, enabled the project to focus more clearly on the needs of teachers in the second phase.

This was given added relevance by the growing recognition that for teachers to be effective in EMU they had to be comfortable with the emotive and affective aspects of learning. At the same time, QPEP's research illustrated the fact that stress was often the most pressing issue for teachers, and that any INSET provision from QPEP had to reduce stress to be credible. In a sense the acid test was whether teachers were able to incorporate individual activities in the classroom. Although not curriculum specific, the booklet of conflict resolution skills, "Wee People", that QPEP produced was a popular resource for teachers. The lack of production of curriculum materials - although never an expressed aim of the original project - was a key issue that galvanised the promoters of the follow up project "the EMU promoting school" to have this as a target in its first three years.

Throughout the project the role of volunteers was critical, and brought with it strengths, particularly in establishing a rapport with young people, and weaknesses inasmuchas volunteers were perceived by teachers as being young and casually dressed. For their part the volunteers, several of whom had negative experiences of schooling, did not make easy allies of teachers. Nevertheless the sheer commitment, energy, enthusiasm, and professionalism of the volunteers helped to overcome initial resistance.

As the project progressed it built up such a level of confidence and competence amongst its volunteers that new volunteers joining the work were able to enter at a higher level. For some volunteers it felt like being thrown in the deep end, but there was a consistent feeling that the antidote to the feeling of "not knowing it well enough" was learning by doing it. Invariably volunteers gained confidence, and usually found their skills were relevant to other areas of paid work, some going on to get jobs as a result.

The international dimension of the volunteers particularly evident by the regular placement of Eirene volunteers with the project , was appreciated by the children in particular. This international influence was furthered by the work that QPEP did in Israel, Germany, Belgium, Byleorus, Uganda and elsewhere.

Leading an experimental, experiential project, led to tensions between volunteers and staff becoming a source of conflict. This was not anticipated at the outset. Mechanisms for dealing with internal conflict need to be built into the structure and day to day running of any future project continuing this work. It may be a counsel of perfection, but the idea of "remaining with a conflict" until it is dealt with is at the heart of peace education.

A key role of QPEP was to support teachers, and throughout the project it did endeavour to elicit the thinking of teachers, and explore the rationale for the variety of responses it got. The issue of "control", and the apparent lack of it in a classroom workshop was one of the recurring issues that was flagged early in the life of the project. Almost inevitably children found themselves being mandated to attend workshops, this was not so much a problem with younger children for whom the novelty made up for the compulsory nature. Sixth formers, particularly those for whom QPEP was at best a second choice activity, took more time to come round.

In the first years of the project, QPEP was so pleased to get a foot in the door of schools, that it would respond positively to all requests from schools. The first series of workshops it did set the tone for the rest of the project, and the supportof the schools involved helped to encourage the work further.

Andrew Young and the Ulster Quaker Peace Committee as sponsors of the project enabled the staff and volunteers to concentrate on developing the work, without the worry of raising funds. The second phase of the project brought European recognition through the PSEP funding.

By the end of the first phase QPEP had developed a reputation for delivering conflict resolution skills workshops, and it could afford to be proactive in developing partnerships. One school where it was to explore a whole school approach was the newly opened Oakgrove Integrated Primary School. It was in a position to explore new avenues, such as using older children to work with younger children.

Research became more structured, ensuring that individual workshops in a series were evaluated in such a way as to impact on the subsequent workshops, taking into account but not being constrained by, for example, the expressed fears of the teachers.

A major event in the second phase of the project was the ENCORE summer school, which illustrated QPEP's ability to take on something new, and create a dialogue in the process, in this instance between practitioner, academic and policymaker. For some participants there would have been more merit in opportunities to share difficulties, rather than attending workshops that were familiar, or at a skills level they had already achieved.

Although the ENCORE summer school was to be a shop window for a number of workshops particularly appreciated by practising teachers, it was only towards the latter part of the project, with the extensive impact of the pilot peer mediation project that teachers became actively involved in the development of QPEP's work. Arising out of the ENCORE summer school was the link with Manchester Development Education Project's Values and Visions project which was to form the basis of one of the two strands of the EMU Promoting School Project.

The aspect of QPEP's work which was to give rise to the most soul searching was its role in developing the work of NCBI in Northern Ireland. Two years into the project, research was suggesting that QPEP and teachers modify the NCBI model to suit their needs. The overall evaluation spoke of a heavy reliance on NCBI. The debate epitomised the growing awareness within N Ireland generally of the tendency for US models to be prescriptive rather than elicitive, and the challenge that presented.

The need for training to take cognisance of where participants are starting from, particularly where the process engenders strong feelings, and for participants and trainers alike to be clear about their mutual expectations, is paramount. The experience of playing a leading role in developing NCBI work in N Ireland gave QPEP an opportunity to reflect on and research into the nature of resistance to experiential approaches, particularly among teachers.

The Joseph Rowntree Charitable Trust's concern that the CES Evaluation of QPEP should look at the impact of the organisation, helped ensure that the evaluation focussed on strategy for the future. As a result of the evaluation's far reaching recommendations, an internal consultation and one with external organisations led to a proposal for future funding for a new project. In 1994 the Positive Ethos Trust was set up to sponsor the "EMU promoting school" project. The latter will continue, in a more focussed way, the work that QPEP began. Conflict resolution skills training will have peer mediation as an end result, and INSET training will have as a goal the enhancement of EMU at the heart of the school ethos. Funding is being sought for a three year project. It is yet to become clear whether QPEP's body of expertise in education internationally will be made use of by INCORE.

The new project, which is also an action research project at the Centre for the Study of Conflict, will have more involvement of teachers at staff level. It will have as a target the trialling and production of a package centred on the curriculum. The process of developing this will be optimised by ongoing self-evaluation to ensure that targets are reached.

A management committee will be established with a clear mandate, and an explicit lines of communication.

In a very real sense although the Ulster Quaker Peace Education Project came to an end in December 1994, the full effect of its influence as an action research project is in the legacy it leaves in the form of the EMU Promoting School Project.

APPENDIX   1
Management Committee

Felicity Boyd	Secretary
John Darby	Until 1990
Seamus Dunn	From 1991
Robert Gavin	
John Lampen	Chairperson until 1992
John Murray	
Alex McEwen	Chairperson from 1992
Norman Richardson	
Stephen Ryan	

Staff

Full-Time

Jerry Tyrrell	Field Worker	(1988 - 1991)
	Director	(1991 - 1994)
Eileen Healy	Workshop Facilitator	(1991 - 1994)
Sharon Moran	Resources Administrator	(1991 - 1994)

Part-time Action for Community Employment (ACE) Posts

Diane Greer	Workshop Facilitator	(1989)
Bridie Hannigan	Workshop Facilitator	(1989 - 1990)
Majella Harkin	Resources Administrator	(1990)
Sharon Moran	Resources Administrator	(1990 - 1991)
William Pegg	Workshop Facilitator	(1990 - 1991)

BA Peace & Conflict Studies - 3rd year Students on Placement

John Lindsay	(Jan 1989 - Jun 1989)
Marian McClintock	(Jan 1990 - Jun 1990)
Pearse McGranaghan	(Jan 1991 - Jun 1991)
Miriam Sulimain	(Feb 1993 - Jun 1993)
Annette Millar	(Feb 1994 - Jun 1994)

APPENDIX 2

QPEP Team - Volunteer Facilitators

Herbert Andres	(1989 - 1990)	Markus Karcher	(1991 - 1994)
Ursula Birthistle	(1988 - 1993)	Gerry Kennedy	(1988 - 1991)
Jan Caspers	(1991 - 1994)	Susanne Klinker	(1990 - 1991)
Mary Connors	(1991 - 1993)	John Lampen	(1988 - 1994)
Seamus Farrell	(1992 - 1994)	Jackie McCafferty	(1990 - 1991)
Tanya Gallagher	(1990 - 1993)	Peter McCloskey	(1989 - 1991)
Diane Greer	(1988 - 1989)	Paddy O'Hagan	(1988 - 1989)
James Greer	(1988 - 1989)	Lorraine O'Neill	(1992 - 1993)
Bridie Hannigan	(1988 - 1989)	William Pegg	(1991 - 1992)
Majella Harkin	(1988 - 1989)	Helena Schlindwein	(1990 - 1993)
Paul Harvey	(1988 - 1992)	Rainer Schultz	(1993 - 1994)
Eileen Healy	(1990 - 1991)	Günter Zittel	(1992 - 1993)

with
Bronagh Fagan
Tara Gallagher
Diana Lampen
Peter McCarron
Paul McLaughlin
Jane Mountain
Matt Regan
Craig Smallbone

APPENDIX 3
PUBLICATIONS

QPEP Publications

Conflict Busters - A guide to Mediation in Schools	*by John Lampen*
Different Beliefs - Out of Print	*by John Lindsay*
Prejudice Reduction - A Workshop Approach	*by Will Pegg*
Submission to Initiative '92	*by QPEP Team*
Wee People	*by Eileen Healy*

Annual Reports

The Ulster Quaer Peace Education Project Annual Report -
a) 1988-89. b). 1989-90 c). 1990-91 d). 1991-92 e). 1992-93 f). 1993-94

Dissertations

The NCBI Prejudice Reduction Model - teachers' resistance in N. Ireland
[MA Dissertation, University of Ulster,1991]
by Jerry Tyrrell

Contribution to books

"The Ulster Quaker Peace Education Project" *by John Lampen and
Seamus Farrell*
in Countering Bullying, Edited by Delwyn Tatum & Graham Herbert,
Trentham Press 1993
"Mediation & Conciliation Agencies" *by Jerry Tyrrell and Derick Wilson*
in Facets of the Conflict in N. Ireland, Edited by Seamus Dunn, Macmillan
1995
Affirmation Activities *by Jerry Tyrrell*
in Children Working for Peace, to be published by UNICEF

Books

The Peace Kit *by John Lampen*
Published by Quaker Home Service

Articles

"Affirmation, Communication and Co-Operation" *by Jerry Tyrrell*
in CRC Journal Issue 5 Winter 1993/94
"Mediating the Irish Conflict" *by Jerry Tyrrell and Terry Duffy*
in Reconciliation Quarterly Summer 1994
"Reflections on Mediation in the context of Empathy" *by Jerry Tyrrell* in
The Fourth R, Volume 53 Oct/Nov 1994